MW00334475

PRODUCED BY:

I like this grape.

VOICE OF MODERN WINE CULTURE

ILIKETHISGRAPE.COM

AUTHOR
PAUL HODGINS

DESIGNER
KATHY LAJVARDI

SERIES EDITOR
NAUSHAD HUDA

↳

DRIVE THROUGH NAPA

TABLE OF CONTENTS

CHAPTER

01:

PG. 13

INTRODUCTION

02:

PG. 23

A BRIEF HISTORY OF
WINE IN CALIFORNIA

03:

PG. 35

CALIFORNIA'S
WINE REGIONS

04:

PG. 41

NAPA VALLEY

05:

PG. 53

NAPA'S 16 AVAS

NAPA'S SUB-AVAs

SOUTH TO NORTH

NAPA'S SUB-AVAs

SOUTH TO NORTH

AVA 1	CARNEROS	PG. 59
AVA 2	COOMBSVILLE	PG. 73
AVA 3	WILD HORSE VALLEY	PG. 87
AVA 4	MOUNT VEEDER	PG. 95
AVA 5	OAK KNOLL	PG. 109
AVA 6	YOUNTVILLE	PG. 123
AVA 7	STAGS LEAP	PG. 137
AVA 8	ATLAS PEAK	PG. 151
AVA 9	OAKVILLE	PG. 165
AVA 10	RUTHERFORD	PG. 179
AVA 11	CHILES VALLEY	PG. 193
AVA 12	ST. HELENA	PG. 201
AVA 13	SPRING MOUNTAIN	PG. 215
AVA 14	HOWELL MOUNTAIN	PG. 229
AVA 15	DIAMOND MOUNTAIN	PG. 243
AVA 16	CALISTOGA	PG. 257

THANKS!

When we started this project we assumed there would be reams of information out there that would make our job a breeze. No such luck. Napa's AVAs, especially the newer ones, are surprisingly under-analyzed.

Instead, we resorted to good old journalism: visiting places, interviewing experts and trying to piece together as much information as we could from countless disparate sources.

Many people and organizations were crucial to our work.

The winemakers and winery owners who consented to be interviewed for this book have made it infinitely more valuable and interesting. As you will see, their passion and expertise come through in equal measure.

Julie Kodmur was a source of information and inspiration. Few people share her level of overall knowledge or enthusiasm about winemaking in Napa Valley.

Daniel de Polo, President of Darioush Wines, shared his encyclopedic knowledge of Napa with us. He also introduced us to Andy Erickson, legendary Napa Valley winemaker.

▼

Napa Valley Vintners generously supplied detailed data about Napa's AVAs, and *Korinne Munson*, the group's director of communications, cheerfully complied with our many requests.

Heini Zachariassen, founder of *Vivino*, provided us with advice and data to create detailed price-to-value charts.

Christie Dufault, Professor of Wine & Beverage at the Culinary Institute of America, graciously agreed to proofread some vital passages on short notice.

Two wine industry professionals also provided assistance: *Gretchen Brakesman*, Executive Director, Spring Mountain District Association; and *Nancy Bialek*, Executive Director, Stags Leap District Winegrowers.

Additional thanks go to *Julie Lim*, owner of the OC Wine Mart & Tasting Bar; *Brenda Lhormer*, cofounder of the Napa Valley Film Festival; and *Anne Valdespino*, food writer for The Orange County Register.

Naushad and Kathy would like to thank their kids *Aara* and *Nouri* for their patience while we were going through the process of this project. Also, we salute the *Huda* and *Lajvardi* families for their ongoing support and love for our cray-cray ideas!

CHAPTER

01:

INTRODUCTION

INTRODUCTION

DRIVE THROUGH NAPA

CALIFORNIA

NAPA VALLEY

Wine is as much a part of California's identity as Hollywood, surfing and perfect weather.

Anyone who wants to understand the history, economy, culture and epicurean tastes of the Golden State should study its world of wine.

CONSIDER →

IT'S A HUGE INDUSTRY.

If California were a country, it would be the world's fourth largest wine producer.

There are almost 4,700 wineries and more than 100 wine-producing regions peppered throughout the state.

In 2017, California wine accounted for $35.2 billion in domestic sales; 90 percent of America's $1.5 billion in wine exports that year were produced in California.

4,700
wineries

100
wine-producing regions

▼

WINE HAS BEEN MADE IN CALIFORNIA FOR A LONG TIME.

Spanish missionaries brought winemaking to California in the mid-1700s, long before it became a state.

European settlers established quality vineyards in many parts of the state by the mid-1800s.

IT'S BEEN A KEY PLAYER IN THE WINE WORLD FOR MORE THAN A CENTURY.

Californians were making and exporting world-class wines in the last two decades of the 19th century, and California's vineyards were crucial to revitalizing European vineyards after disease ravaged the Old World's crops in the late 1800s.

▼

IT'S STILL GROWING LIKE CRAZY.

The number of California wineries doubled between 1998 and 2006, and doubled again in the following decade. In 2016, California produced more than 680 million gallons of wine, about 85 percent of total U.S. output.

1998

2006

2016

SO HOW DOES THE AVERAGE WINE LOVER APPROACH SUCH A GARGANTUAN TOPIC?

BY USING THIS HANDY GUIDE.

We make it easy for you to find the facts you need, the regions that pique your interest, and the wines that strike your fancy. Our compact, readable and well-researched books cover California's wine universe succinctly, accurately, and with maximum clarity. Whether you read it at home, on the plane, in the car or on the wine trail, the Drive Through series aims to give you just what you need.

WINE TERMS

ALLUVIAL FAN:
A fan- or cone-shaped deposit of sediment crossed and built up by streams, sometimes very deep; alluvial soil is common in Napa.

AMERICAN VITICULTURAL AREA (AVA):
A designated wine grape-growing region in the United States distinguishable by features of geography, soil, and climate. Its boundaries must be approved by the Alcohol and Tobacco Tax and Trade Bureau.

BORDEAUX BLEND:
The six red grapes grown in Bordeaux are Cabernet Sauvignon, Cabernet Franc and Merlot, and in lesser amounts, Carménère, Malbec and Petit Verdot. They are customarily blended.

DIURNAL SWING:
The difference between the daytime high temperature and the nighttime low in a specific location. A wide diurnal swing is an asset for most grapes.

FIELD BLEND:
More than one grape variety planted together in the same vineyard. All the grapes are harvested at the same time and made into wine together.

▼

OLD WORLD:
In viticulture, the wine producing areas of Europe.

PHENOLIC CONTENT:
A group of several hundred chemical compounds present in grapes that affect the taste, color and mouth feel of wine.

PHYLLOXERA:
A small bug that destroys the rootstalk of Old World grapevines. A worldwide phylloxera epidemic in the late 19th century decimated the wine industry.

PROHIBITION:
An era between 1920 and 1933 when the production, importation, transportation and sale of alcoholic beverages in the U.S. were prohibited. It almost brought domestic wine production to a halt.

ROOTSTALK:
A horizontal stem with shoots above and roots below that is the reproductive structure for grapevines.

VERAISON:
The onset of ripening, when the grapes change from green to red and begin to sweeten and grow.

VITICULTURE:
The cultivation of grape vines.

CHAPTER

02:

A BRIEF HISTORY OF
WINE IN CALIFORNIA

▼

THE CATHOLIC CHURCH ANCHORS THE INDUSTRY

In California, wine and the Catholic Church are as tightly intertwined as two ancient grape vines. The state's celebrated wine industry owes a huge debt to the Church's agricultural practices and customs during the Mission period (1769-1834). And if it weren't for Catholicism's perpetual need for sacramental wine, California's winemaking industry might have withered completely during Prohibition.

Spanish missionaries brought the first rootstalk to the untamed region in the middle of the 18th century. As the mission system crept inexorably north along the Camino Real, a path that always stayed within a few miles of the California coast, grapes were planted immediately at each new mission, mainly for the purpose of making wine.

Historians have determined that the first vineyard in what would become California was planted around 1779 at the inaugural mission, San Diego de Alcalá, in present-day San Diego; the premiere vintage was likely 1782. Coastal California's Mediterranean climate – warm, dry summers and mild winters with significant rain – were perfect for many kinds of southern European grapes, particularly those of Italy, Spain and southern France.

The preferred wine of the time would probably not find favor with connoisseurs today: sweet, often fortified with alcohol, it could be as strong as port or sherry. Nevertheless it was in high demand, particularly from the Church. Saint Junipero Serra, the architect of the mission system, complained that the missions often struggled to produce enough wine for the celebration of the Mass.

The Mission grape is shrouded in mystery. There is disagreement about its origins, although it probably came to the New World from Spain. Some think it was interbred with the pink Criolla grape from Argentina and Chile's red País grape. It was better for sweet, fortified wines and brandy than high-quality dry wines.

▼

BOOM, BUST, REBIRTH

After the Mission period ended, winemaking outside the supervision of the Church grew in popularity. Many of the early winemaking families emigrated from Catholic countries and regions; most hailed from France or parts of what would later become Germany and Italy. They were familiar with the processes and rules governing the making of altar wine. Buena Vista, Krug, Gundlach Bundschu and other commercial wineries of the time undoubtedly provided wine for the Catholic Church, although the evidence is largely anecdotal.

By the 1880s, California boasted a large wine industry with a global reach, and California wines were beginning to win prestigious European competitions. Almost 300 grape varieties were being grown in the state's wineries.

But the California wine industry was soon felled by two disasters. One was conjured by nature, a destructive pest called phylloxera, which we'll discuss later. The other disaster was man-made: Prohibition.

In December 1918, after intense lobbying by well-established temperance organizations, the 18th Amendment was proposed by the U.S. Senate. It prohibited the "manufacture, sale, or transportation of intoxicating liquors for beverage purposes."

In January 1919 the amendment achieved the necessary two-thirds majority of state ratification, and selling booze in the U.S. became a crime when the country officially went dry on Jan. 17, 1920.

The Volstead Act, passed in October 1919 over President Woodrow Wilson's veto, gave the law teeth with provisions for enforcement and the formation of a new special unit within the Treasury Department.

The American wine industry was obliterated. Before 1920, the U.S. was home to more than 2,500 commercial wineries. Fewer than 100 survived the era of Prohibition, which lasted until 1933. Making wine for the Catholic Church was the principal source of income for many of them.

But those dark days contained a silver lining: the Church helped form the foundation for the modern California wine industry.

Brother Timothy Diener, a faculty member at the Institute of the Brothers of the Christian Schools, was transferred in 1935 to the order's Mont La Salle in Napa Valley's Mount Veeder region. While there he became a wine chemist and helped the order's already-established wine business. The Christian Brothers had provided sacramental wine during Prohibition, and under Brother Timothy's guidance the winery thrived as a quality commercial producer. It was considered one of the nation's finest wineries in those years.

▼

THE MONDAVI EFFECT

It took time for the California wine industry to recover from Prohibition. Until the early 1960s, the state was known mainly as a producer of sweet port-style wines made from Carignan and Thompson Seedless grapes. But quality winemaking was still practiced, mainly by some of the well-established European families in Napa, Sonoma and on the Central Coast. Table wines sales finally overtook fortified wines in 1968, regaining the status of most popular wine category. California had 713 bonded wineries before Prohibition; it took more than 65 years, until 1986, before that many were again operating.

Around the same time, multi-generational winemaking families (as well as a few newcomers) began to explore the world of premium wine, especially in Napa and Sonoma. Names such as Mondavi, Heitz and David Bruce became nationally known.Cabernet Sauvignon became the quality grape of choice, and European concepts such as estate wine, terroir, varietal and geographic designation, and proper Bordeaux blends took root. Collaboration between respected European houses and American wineries began at this point as well, another sign that California was beginning to be recognized as a place with potential.

A crucial catalyst in these formative postwar decades was Russian-born winemaker and consultant Andre Tchelistcheff, whose contributions helped shape the style of California's best wines, especially Cabernet Sauvignon, and whose advice influenced several generations of winemakers. (More on him later.)

As the quality of California wine improved, critics and retailers were forced to take notice. A breakthrough occurred in 1976 when British wine merchant Steven Spurrier hosted a blind taste test in Paris that pitted several California wineries against well-respected labels from Bordeaux and Burgundy. The Californians shockingly won both red and white categories at the event, which came to be known as "The Judgment of Paris." From that point forward, California's wine could not be denied. The birth of the American Viticultural Area (AVA) designation was another sign of the American wine industry's increasing maturity.

An AVA can be any size (there are no minimums or maximums) and may even cross state or county lines. Many of us are familiar with the major wine growing regions such as Napa and Sonoma, but within each there may be many appellations, both large and small. A few of them have vineyards but no wineries. In Napa and elsewhere, many "nested" AVAs can be found inside other AVAs. Later we'll look more closely at how the AVA designation system works, together with its challenges and complications.Napa Valley was California's first AVA. Established in 1981, the Napa AVA is now home to 16 nested appellations.

▼

21ST-CENTURY DEVELOPMENTS

In the last two decades, a new generation of winemakers have brought university training and a more scientific approach to their craft. Many are graduates of well-respected programs at UC Davis, Cal Poly in San Luis Obispo and California State University, Fresno.

THEY HAVE EMBRACED SOPHISTICATED TECHNOLOGIES TO ANALYZE PHENOLIC CONTENT, HYDROLOGY, AND OTHER SCIENTIFIC ASPECTS OF THE WINEMAKER'S WORLD.

Some of these winemakers show a curiosity for unorthodox techniques in the vineyard and the winery. Organic farming is becoming more common; so is biodynamic winemaking, despite its sometimes controversial practices.

Over the last generation, Napa and Sonoma have gradually lost their dominance as newer California wine regions came under vine and began to produce quality wine. Central and Southern California finally shed the stigma of being too hot, as young and adventurous winemakers discovered a universe of microclimates, some of them quite cool, stretching from south of Monterey Bay all the way to the Mexican border.

Regions north of Napa and Sonoma have also begun to produce quality wine, especially areas near the coast and, less commonly, in the Sierra foothills.

LODI
ANDERSON VALLEY
SANTA LUCIA HIGHLANDS
PASO ROBLES
SANTA YNEZ VALLEY

– all are now respected as places where quality wine is made.

▼

MORE THAN 100 VARIETIES OF GRAPE ARE NOW GROWN IN CALIFORNIA.

Trends dictate the waxing and waning of a particular grape's appeal; productive vineyards have been routinely ripped out after their grape lost its popularity.

(If there'd been no obsession with white Zinfandel in the 1980s there might have been no red Zinfandel resurgence – it was very un-trendy for a time.)

At the moment, the seven most popular varieties statewide are:

CABERNET SAUVIGNON
CHARDONNAY
MERLOT
PINOT NOIR
SAUVIGNON BLANC
SYRAH
ZINFANDEL

WRITE NOTES HERE:

CHAPTER

03:

CALIFORNIA'S WINE REGIONS

▼

YOU CAN FIND WINE REGIONS ALL OVER CALIFORNIA.

Some, like Napa and Sonoma, are universally recognized and quite accessible. Others are tucked away in more obscure corners of the Golden State, though it's often a visually stunning adventure to drive there.

One thing wine fans find confusing about California is that latitude isn't as important as proximity to the ocean in determining climate. While the Santa Rita Hills AVA is more than 300 miles south of Napa, it's one of the coolest wine regions in the state thanks to the east-west orientation of its hilly topography, which creates an intense marine influence from the cool North Pacific Ocean.

Microclimates are everywhere — that's why Windward Vineyard makes nothing but Pinot Noir even though its vineyards are in the middle of a warm region west of Paso Robles. A small dip in the landscape around Windward's vineyards provides a well of chilly air that's perfect for that cool-climate grape.

▼

Altitude also plays a crucial role in California's wine world. The temperature drops 3.5 degrees Fahrenheit for every 1,000 feet of elevation gain. A 90-degree day at sea level would be just 78 degrees in a vineyard planted 3,500 feet above.

CALIFORNIA IS GEOLOGICALLY DIVERSE, AND THAT PLAYS AN IMPORTANT ROLE IN VITICULTURE.

From the rich, deep alluvial plains of Lodi to the chalky white calcareous formations west of Paso Robles, geology and soil composition determine crucial elements such as water retention.

GEOLOGY

SOIL

WEATHER

▼

RAINFALL CAN BE SURPRISINGLY VARIED IN WINE COUNTRY.

Some larger wine regions experience a difference of 50 inches a year or more from wettest to driest parts. California's many mountains, hills, valleys and gorges create localized rain shadows and wet micro-climates. And the increasingly profound drought cycles throughout the American West place growing emphasis on dry farming and the careful husbanding of water resources.

California's recent bout of unreliable rainfall is one of the reasons that dry farming is becoming more common. Grapes can be remarkably drought-tolerant compared to other commercial crops, and the general consensus is that a stressed-out grape makes better wine. That's why many growers practice the "bathtub" curve method of irrigation, providing more water at the beginning and end of the fruit's annual cycle and parching it in the middle months. Nutrient-poor soils are becoming ever more prized for vineyards, too. Nothing is worse for a promising wine grape than abundance.

Every bottle of California wine on the market notes its geographical origin. If the grapes are sourced from a number of different places within the state's borders, it could be listed as the state of California itself. The label could also indicate a county within the state.

For a wine to carry an AVA designation, at least 85 percent of the grapes must be grown within that AVA. If a county is listed on the label, that number is 75 percent. And any wine with the "California" designation indicates that 100 percent of the grapes in that bottle were grown in the Golden State.

Varietal designations are the names of the dominant grapes used in the wine: Cabernet Sauvignon, Chardonnay, Zinfandel, etc. A varietal designation on the label signifies that at least 75 percent of the grapes used to make the wine are of that variety, and the entire 75 percent was grown in the labeled area.

"Estate Bottled" means that 100 percent of the wine was made from grapes grown on land owned and controlled by the winery. The winery is required to crush and ferment the grapes and finish, age, and bottle the wine in a continuous process on its own premises. The winery and the vineyard must be in the same AVA.

Drive Through Napa, the first book in the series, looks exclusively at California's most celebrated wine region, Napa Valley.

CHAPTER

04:

NAPA VALLEY

▼

789 SQUARE MILES
16 AVAS
600+ WINERIES

Although easily the most famous wine region in California, Napa Valley produces just four percent of all California wine. Only 30 miles long and five miles from side to side at its widest point, it's home to 16 AVAs, more than 600 wineries, 46,000 vineyard acres, and some of the finest wines in the country. Napa's AVAs can be divided roughly into two categories, valley floor and hillside (though there's intermingling between the two on some properties). The most sought-after AVAs include Carneros, Howell Mountain, Mount Veeder, Oakville, Rutherford, Stags Leap District and Yountville. But many other appellations are gaining ground as newer AVAs become more deeply understood by grape growers and winemakers.

Along the west side of Napa County are the Mayacamas Mountains, home to Mount St. Helena, at 4,344 feet the second tallest peak in the area. The range stretches for 52 miles in a northwest-to-southeast direction. The east side of the valley is bounded by the Vaca Mountains.

These hills might not seem tall, but they can have an outsized effect on microclimates, which are everywhere in Napa. They play a crucial part in fog patterns, average temperatures, seasonal variations, and diurnal swing.

The 55-mile-long Napa River flows south-southeast down the valley. It begins as seasonal Kimball Canyon Creek in Robert Louis Stevenson State Park, following the southern slope of Mt. St. Helena to Kimball Canyon Dam, and enters the narrow northern end of Napa Valley north of Calistoga. In the valley bottom, the river meanders past Calistoga, St. Helena, Rutherford, and Oakville and widens considerably in the city of Napa. A few miles downstream it empties into a tidal estuary, meeting the ocean at the eastern edge of San Pablo Bay.

Napa is notably warmer in the summer months than its larger neighbor to the west, Sonoma County. Surprisingly, its northern reaches are significantly hotter than most of Santa Barbara County, more than 300 miles to the south. The cooling effect of San Pablo Bay decreases steadily as you travel north.

Napa is best known for Cabernet Sauvignon (it represents about half of all vineyard acreage) and other red Bordeaux varieties, but the area also produces fine Chardonnay, Merlot, Pinot Noir, Sauvignon Blanc, Riesling and Zinfandel. Over the years many Old World grapes have been planted here, but unlike Europe, Napa and the rest of California have tended to follow the forces of fashion; several varieties that were hugely popular a century or even 50 years ago are rare today.

Grape growing has been practiced in the small valley since Mission times, but the Gold Rush brought the pioneers who laid the foundation for commercial winemaking. By the early 1860s, European immigrants had established themselves as farmers, grape growers and winemakers in the areas between San Francisco and gold country.

▼

Zinfandel, often called "California's grape," was introduced during the Gold Rush, becoming widely planted in many parts of the state during the mid-1850s. A hardy and adaptable grape that's closely related to Italy's Primitivo and Crljenak Kastelanski, an ancient Croatian variety, Zinfandel thrived all over the Golden State, and it played an important role in Napa before Prohibition.

Today it's the third-leading wine grape variety statewide, with more than 44,400 acres planted and 416,615 tons crushed in 2016, according to the California Department of Food and Agriculture. Zin is grown in 45 of California's 58 counties and enjoys a huge cult following, as anyone who's attended a rowdy ZAP (Zinfandel Associates & Producers) gathering can attest. Although it is still found in Napa, Zin is not as desirable or commercially significant these days as Cabernet Sauvignon and other Bordeaux grapes in the valley.

California wine came into its own between 1860 and 1880.

In 1860, businessman John Patchett planted winemaking vineyards and hired Prussian immigrant Charles Krug to make wine using the technology and materials then available – the wine presses and barrels were made of cedar and other local wood in that era.

Germans populated the industry in the 1860s and '70s. Joseph Schram planted California's first hillside vineyard in 1862, the same year he founded Schramsberg Winery.

Nearby, Jacob Beringer and his brother bought 215 acres of land in Napa in 1875, founding Beringer, considered to be Napa's oldest continuously operating winery.

Gustave Niebaum, a Finnish-born sea captain of Swedish descent who had become one of the world's most successful fur traders by 1870, was ready to sink a chunk of his immense fortune into French winemaking. But a few of Niebaum's business partners had been successfully growing wine grapes in Napa Valley for almost a decade. And his wife, a German-American California girl, wanted him to invest closer to home. A few years after they married in 1873, the Niebaums bought about 450 acres of Napa land and started planting wine grapes.

An ingenious Niebaum employee named Hamden McIntyre, self-trained as an architect and engineer, designed America's first gravity-flow wineries for his boss and several other pioneering winemakers during the 1880s. (Using gravity rather than pumps to move wine during different production stages is gentler on the fruit.) Such new techniques and technology brought a sudden and dramatic improvement in quality, and the modern era of California winemaking was born. By the early 1880s, after two decades of increasingly successful large-scale winemaking, Napa was becoming one of the world's major hubs for commercial wine production. A few of its wineries regularly won prestigious prizes at European contests.

This tremendous leap was followed by an equally dramatic backslide – actually, two of them. The first was terrible news not only for the Napa Valley but for wineries in the rest of the U.S. and Europe.

East of the Rocky Mountains, a tiny yellow aphid-like bug called phylloxera laid waste to imported grapevines by sucking the life out of their root system. Most grape species that were native to North America had become immune to the minuscule pest. Unfortunately, the vines of Europe had no natural defenses against phylloxera.

Phylloxera began its journey of destruction in California by infecting the defenseless Mission vines, the otherwise hardy Old World grapes imported by Spain for use in its mission vineyards. By 1872, European grapes in Sonoma and Napa were deeply affected – not surprising since the main Mission-era road, Camino Real, led through Sonoma County.

Meanwhile, native American species of grapevines were sent to Europe, along with their destructive little hitchhikers. The phylloxera epidemic first appeared in French vineyards in the late 1860s.

By the mid-1870s the infection was worldwide in scope, and there was no apparent cure. Grape growers tried every trick they could think of – poison gas, flooding – without result.

Eventually, ingenious plant biologists made a fortuitous discovery. An Old World grapevine grafted to the rootstalk of a phylloxera-resistant North American variety was the answer. The superior fruit remained the same, and the New World root system was impervious to the bugs.

▼

But it took time to reset the industry. It meant pulling up most pre-infestation grapevines in Europe and California, and it wasn't a perfect solution. Phylloxera continued to appear in Napa well into the 20th century, and many acres of vineyards were planted to other commercial crops.

Before the industry had fully recovered, another disaster struck in the 1920s and early '30s, this one man-made: Prohibition (see chapter 1). More vineyards and wineries were abandoned over those 14 years, leaving only a few Napa stalwarts such as Chateau Montelena to subsist, mainly by producing sacramental wines for the Catholic Church.

With the repeal of Prohibition in 1933, Napa Valley's wine industry began its slow and halting journey back to health. John Daniel Jr. brought back Inglenook, one of 19th-century Napa's most famous names. Georges de Latour revived Beaulieu Vineyards (BV).

Talented new arrivals began to leave their marks: Louis M. Martini and a hard-working clan named Mondavi (pronounced with a long "A" in those days), who purchased Charles Krug Winery and started making sturdy low-priced wine.

Around this time, Napa's game changer appeared: André Tchelistcheff.

Born in Moscow in 1901 to an aristocratic family (his father was Chief Justice of the Russian Imperial Court), Tchelistcheff barely survived the Russian Revolution and Civil War as an officer (he was left for dead on a snow-covered Crimean battlefield in 1921 after an ambush).

He studied agricultural technology in Czechoslovakia before moving to France, where he rose to prominence as an oenologist at the Institut Pasteur and the Institut National Agronomique.

Hired by Beaulieu Vineyards founder and owner Georges de Latour in 1938, Tchelistcheff became a seminal and universally honored figure in the California wine industry. Tchelistcheff introduced many new techniques and procedures to California such as aging wine in small French oak barrels, cold fermentation, vineyard frost prevention and malolactic fermentation. He accurately assessed the varieties that would do best throughout the valley, and he was instrumental in advising wineries in other parts of the state during their formative years. He recognized the potential of Paso Robles in the early 1960s and accurately predicted the grape varieties that would thrive there.

The 33 years between the end of Prohibition and the opening of Mondavi's iconic and visitor-friendly wine facility in 1966 are often characterized as a sleepy time for Napa. In reality, it was an era of slow but determined growth and improving quality.

Almost 6,000 acres of wine grapes were planted in the 1940s. Familiar labels established themselves as makers of quality wine: Beaulieu, Beringer, Inglenook, Wente, Concannon. In 1944, seven vintners signed an agreement that formed the Napa Valley Vintners trade association.

In the next generation, several names came to dominate the valley's wine industry.

▼

First among these, of course, was Robert Mondavi. Charming, ambitious, and hard driving, he left his family business at the former Charles Krug winery to form his own label in 1965 with two partners, Ivan Schoch and Fred Holmes. Their initial 12-acre purchase is now the home of the winery, cellars and administrative offices of the Mondavi estate.

Mondavi immediately launched a massive project, building the first major winery in Napa since 1933. The opening of the elegant, mission-inspired building marked the beginning of the modern era of Napa winemaking. Mondavi championed the promotion of single-varietal wine and single-handedly revitalized Sauvignon Blanc. He renamed the unpopular grape "Fume Blanc" and created a new dry, oaky style for the variety in a bold stroke of marketing savvy.

In 1968, Schoch and Holmes sold their shares in the Mondavi winery. Moving quickly, Robert Mondavi bought 230 acres of the legendary To-Kalon vineyard. Over the next 10 years, a partnership between Mondavi and Baron Philippe Rothschild of Chateau Mouton Rothschild led to the creation of Opus One in 1979, a high-end label that took advantage of superior-quality To-Kalon vineyard fruit.

If a single event can be credited with putting Napa Valley on the global wine map, it was the Paris Tasting of May 24, 1976. This comparative contest pitted Cabernet Sauvignon and Chardonnay from California against the best wines of Bordeaux and Burgundy in a blind tasting. When it was done, the judges had given top honors to Chateau Montelena Chardonnay and Stag's Leap Wine Cellars Cabernet Sauvignon. Napa Valley would never be the same.

▼

Napa's "AJP" (after the Judgement of Paris) era has been marked by several crucial developments. In the 1970s, single-vineyard releases were pioneered by Ridge, Heitz Cellars, Diamond Creek and a few other respected labels. Specific vineyard origins began to appear on higher-end wine labels.

Wine critic Robert Parker entered the picture when he founded *The Wine Advocate* in 1978. For the next three decades he was undoubtedly the most influential voice in Napa, and his preferences led to changes in the way wine was being styled. A believer in ripe fruit, low yields, meticulous sorting and the use of new French oak barrels, Parker also graded his opinions on a 100-point scale. It's a system that grew to dominate wine journalism and consumer decision-making, for better or worse.

Parker and the increasingly knowledgeable wine-buying public pushed Napa in new directions. The late 1980s and early 1990s saw an explosion in the number of high-end winemakers, small wineries, and the concept of "hand-crafted" or artisanal wine that was pricey and highly allocated (usually distributed through membership clubs), making it difficult for the general consumer to buy.

This trend dovetailed perfectly with a run of excellent vintages in Napa from 1990-97. In those days, a high rating and words of praise from Parker could catapult a small winery instantly from obscurity to fame.

The other important development of this era was

THE CREATION OF THE AMERICAN VITICULTURAL AREA, OR AVA.

Using Old World practices of territorial designation as its inspiration, the AVA system has succeeded in placing premium value on certain wine-producing regions, some of them quite small.

This practice is being repeated in many other regions of California, with similar results.

CHAPTER

05:

NAPA'S 16 SUB-AVAs

▼

AMERICAN VITICULTURAL AREA

The AVA (American Viticultural Area) designation can be a little confusing and controversial, so let's examine it in detail.

An American Viticultural Area is a wine grape-growing region anywhere in the U.S. that can be defined as unique by evidence of geography, geology, weather and other factors. Its boundaries are set by the Alcohol and Tobacco Tax and Trade Bureau (TTB) of the United States Department of the Treasury.

Additional rules complicate the decision.

THE TTB REQUIRES THE FOLLOWING:

1. Evidence that the name of the proposed new AVA is locally or nationally known as referring to the area.

2. Historical or current evidence that the boundaries are legitimate.

3. Evidence that growing conditions such as climate, soil, elevation and physical features are distinctive.

Petitioners applying for AVA status must provide all that information, as well as USGS maps to clearly show the AVA's proposed boundaries. Once an AVA is established, at least 85 percent of the grapes used to make a wine must be grown in the specified area if an AVA is referenced on its label.

The Napa Valley as a whole is an AVA, designated in 1981. It is California's first recognized AVA and the second in the United States. Within the Napa Valley AVA are 16 nested AVAs (sometimes called sub-appellations or sub-AVAs, though those terms can be confusing as they imply hierarchical relationships):

Atlas Peak, Calistoga, Chiles Valley, Coombsville, Diamond Mountain, Howell Mountain, Carneros, Mt. Veeder, Oak Knoll, Oakville, Rutherford, St. Helena, Spring Mountain, Stags Leap, Yountville and Wild Horse Valley.

As of December 2018, there are 107 American Viticultural Areas in California. This explosion of designations is not universally supported or appreciated.

Many wine industry professionals think 107 are just too many. It took centuries for specially designated wine-producing areas in Europe to develop, based on year after year of uninterrupted wine production and a deep, multigenerational understanding of local ecosystems. France, about 50 percent bigger than California, has more than 300 unique regions (the French use the term appellation d'origine contrôlée, or AOC), but its territorial designation system can be traced back to 1411.

▼

Determining the borders of an AVA is sometimes tainted by politics and favoritism. Being left just outside the boundary of a desirable AVA could mean the difference between thriving and dying for a winery, since AVA designations translate into consumers' buying decisions and ultimately bottle prices. Being included in an AVA simply because of good politicking (rumors of such practices persist) undermines the system's credibility. Wine Searcher succinctly identified the underlying issue in a 2014 article. "The problem with the U.S. AVA system is that no one has ever regulated it in a comprehensive way. We have no national wine or regional product commission and, unlike in Europe, no history of the concept. Heck, 45 percent of the wine labeled 'Champagne' (in the U.S.) is still from California."

Fortunately, Napa is relatively free of such controversies compared to other parts of the state. Its 16 appellations, both big and small, all have enough wineries or vineyards (some just barely) to establish a baseline of characteristics for their region and the ways in which those traits affect the grapes. You will, however, encounter some Napa winemakers who maintain that when it comes to what ends up in your glass, the AVA is less of a determining factor than their own practices, choices and preferences.

Here's a brief description of each appellation in Napa— and, in two cases, an AVA that straddles Napa and another county.

Temperatures are listed in Fahrenheit.

If you are travelling from south to north through Napa on Highway 29, you would encounter its AVAs in this order, keeping in mind that some straddle the highway and others are considerably east or west of the road:

CARNEROS

COOMBSVILLE

WILD HORSE VALLEY

MOUNT VEEDER

OAK KNOLL

YOUNTVILLE

STAGS LEAP

ATLAS PEAK

OAKVILLE

RUTHERFORD

CHILES VALLEY

ST. HELENA

SPRING MOUNTAIN

HOWELL MOUNTAIN

DIAMOND MOUNTAIN

CALISTOGA

SOUTH TO NORTH

AVA 1:

CARNEROS

CARNEROS
WINERIES & VINEYARDS

Artesa
Bouchaine Vineyards
Cuvaison Estate Wines
Domaine Carneros
Domaine Chandon
Etude
Gloria Ferrer
Hudson
Hyde
Madonna Estate
McKenzie Mueller
RD Wines
Saintsbury
Schug
Thomas Michael Cellars
Truchard Vineyards

The wine industry is dynamic. For up-to-date listings, please visit individual AVA websites.

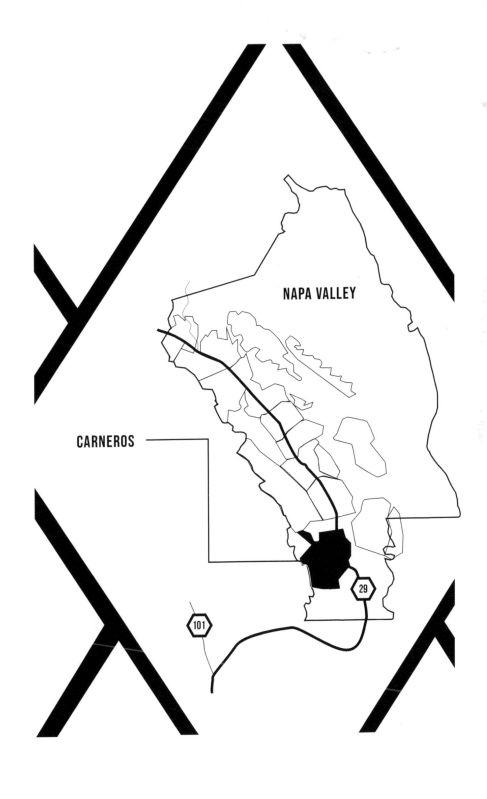

NAPA VALLEY

CARNEROS

101

29

Q & A

CARNEROS

ROMBAUER VINEYARDS

RICHIE ALLEN

AS A WINEMAKER WHAT DO YOU LIKE MOST ABOUT CARNEROS?

Carneros specifically to me is that perfect balance between moderate Mediterranean climate and Continental climate. It sits right at the base of the Napa Valley by the bay. That cool Pacific influence is there, but it's warm enough to ripen fruit.

Every major grape grower here has been in Carneros long enough to make their quality consistent. We work with vineyards that we don't own, but we're very specific about who we work with. It's like dating; you build the relationship. We're half estate and half purchase. About 99 percent of our purchased fruit is long-term contracts. We get exactly what we want.

WHAT EFFECT DOES YOUR REGION HAVE ON THE GRAPES THAT GROW HERE?

When I think of the quintessential California Chardonnay, I swear I can taste the sunshine in it. That's the way I think of Carneros. But because of its proximity to the coast, you get acid too. There are very few places like that in the world where you have a balance of warmth and coolness to ripen the fruit. The challenges are the really cool years. 2011 was like that.

You need to be able to get the fruit ripe enough, which you can do if you manage your canopies. And close to the water, wind can be an issue. Strong evening breezes can really move things around. Mildew is definitely a challenge in Carneros, too. You have these foggy mornings and sunny afternoons that are perfect for mold spores. And the soils here are pretty low in vigor. But all of those challenges give our wines uniqueness. We're quite different than all other parts of Napa.

WHAT WILL WE NOTICE WHEN TASTING A WINE FROM YOUR AVA?

I'd say there is always an attractive ripeness to the fruit. Especially with Chardonnay, there is a noticeable ripeness level. You'll also get crispy lime and lemon curd aroma. And whether it's put through malolactic fermentation or not, the underlying acid is the backbone of the wine. That beautiful acidity, coupled with the ripe fruit and the depth and weight you get from a slightly less cool climate, gives the wine this voluptuous quality. That's what our wine is renowned for.

▼

WHAT DO PEOPLE MISUNDERSTAND ABOUT YOUR AVA?

Honestly, the biggest misconception is that Carneros is in Napa; it's actually in both Napa and Sonoma. We work on both sides and the AVA is in both counties. It is cool by Napa standards – it's the coolest part of the valley. But I wouldn't call it a cool climate like you find in Burgundy. Its proximity to the bay is what drives it, but it can get warm, too. It's the most southern AVA in the valley, right on San Pablo Bay. From one of our vineyards you can see Golden Gate Bridge on a clear day.

Because we're surrounded by water, people make certain wrong assumptions. But the big limiting factor in Carneros is water. Our average rainfall is decent, but we don't dry farm our Chardonnay. There are a lot of ground wells that either contain high boron content or salt from the bay.

AVA 1

CARNEROS

DRIVE THROUGH NAPA

CLIMATE

Cool, with prevailing marine winds from San Pablo Bay and through the Petaluma Gap to the west. High temperatures during summer rarely exceed 80 degrees. Chilliest AVA in Napa or Sonoma.

ELEVATION

Sea level to 700 feet. Most vineyards are found at 400 feet or below.

RAINFALL

Up to 24 inches annually.

SOILS

Clay-dominated, very shallow in general, with more loam and hillside alluvials in the northern section. Yields typically are restrained by the hard clay pan subsoil, which prevents deep rooting.

PRINCIPAL VARIETIES & CHARACTERISTICS

Chardonnay: mineral-ish pear-apple and spice flavors. Merlot: lean and lightly herbal, with fine tannins and sleek structure. Pinot Noir: ripe cherry-cinnamon spice flavors with earthy notes.

▼

Los Carneros, often simply called Carneros, straddles the Napa-Sonoma border, although the lion's share of the district is in Sonoma; it often uses the Sonoma Valley AVA designation as well. Adjacent to San Pablo Bay, it has proven to be an excellent home for Chardonnay and Pinot Noir, and it produces world-class sparkling wines. Designated as an AVA on Aug. 18, 1983, it was the first nested appellation to include Napa (Howell Mountain, designated later that year, was the first AVA contained entirely within Napa).

About 90 square miles in size, Carneros starts along the low-lying hills of the Mayacamas range, and you'll see vineyards extending from sea level to altitudes of 400 feet or more.

The region, like much of the coast around San Francisco, is cool and breezy year-round, with less temperature variation than points farther north; it's the chilliest and windiest AVA in Napa and Sonoma, and it sees significant amounts of fog.

Carneros is known for its unforgiving, thin clay soil, which translates into poor drainage and low fertility for grapevines. Together with the constant wind off the bay, these conditions force the vines to fight to get enough moisture; root systems are shallow, and harvests can be late. While these challenges help to keep crop yields small, they can also delay the grapes from ripening sufficiently. The best vintages feature long growing seasons that allow the fruit to ripen slowly and evenly under consistent conditions.

Not surprisingly, cool-climate varieties such as Pinot Noir and Chardonnay feel right at home here. Many of the grapes grown in Carneros are used for sparkling wine production as well.

▼

Wine producer Louis Martini put Carneros on the wine map in 1942 when he bought the Stanly Ranch and began a massive project to replant vines, choosing the most appropriate varieties for the area and emphasizing quality. By the 1970s, the Carneros region had mushroomed to more than 1,300 acres under vine and was beginning to be known for the quality of its Chardonnays and Pinot Noirs.

Beginning in the 1970s, Mahoney Vineyards' Francis Mahoney and others worked with UC Davis on a long series of clonal experiments to further refine the quality of the area's Pinot Noir.

As Carneros' reputation grew in the wine world, big European houses took notice, and in the 1980s some familiar names moved in and quickly established a presence. Most of them are well-known producers of quality sparkling wine: Domaine Chandon, Domaine Carneros, Gloria Ferrer, Mumm Napa, Codorníu Napa.

The boom waned a bit in the late 1980s, when phylloxera returned to the area and forced many wine producers to plant new vines. But it was a blessing in disguise. Besides planting phylloxera-resistant rootstock, many Carneros producers also experimented with some of the new French clones of Pinot Noir and Chardonnay that were then changing attitudes and winemaking philosophies in France. The Chardonnay boom was a windfall for Carneros, and winemakers responded in kind, eventually planting more than 6,000 acres of that variety by the early 1990s.

In the last 15 years, Carneros has become less rugged and rural. The culinary scene has improved vastly, especially in the downtown riverside area of Napa.

▼

—

PRICE TO RATING CHART

THE GRAPH INDICATES VIVINO USERS' AVERAGE RATINGS FOR WINES AT DIFFERENT PRICE POINTS IN THIS AVA.

DATA POWERED BY VIVINO

CARNEROS

PRICE TO RATING CHART

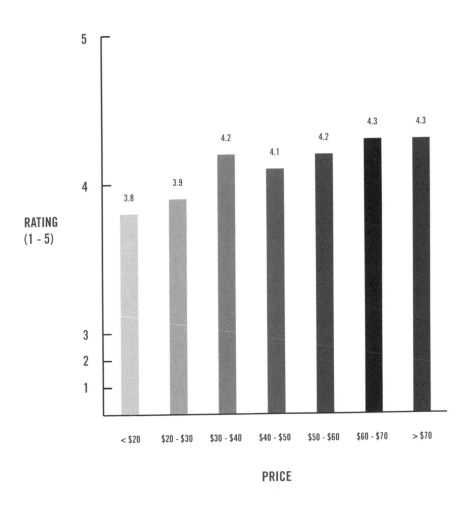

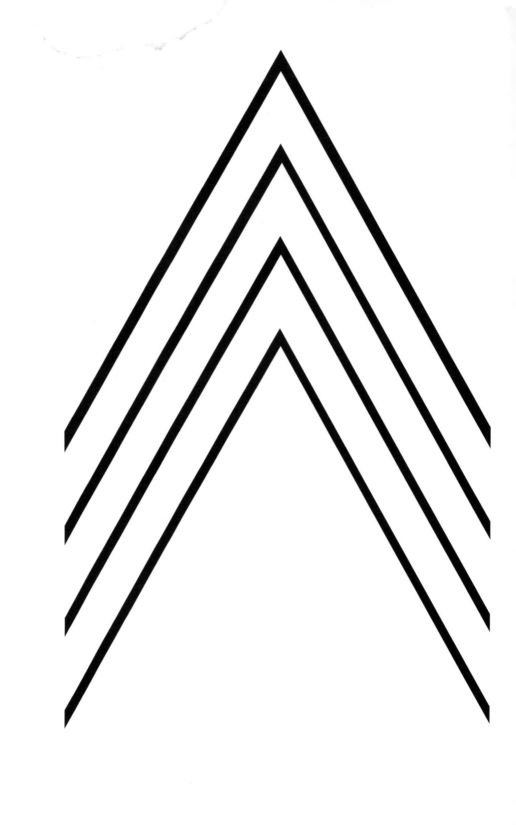

SOUTH TO NORTH

AVA 2:

COOMBSVILLE

COOMBSVILLE
WINERIES & VINEYARDS

Ackerman Family Vineyards
Ancien Wines
Arcadia Vineyards
Arns
Arrow & Branch
Azur Wines
Bennett Vineyards
Black Cat Vineyard
Blue Oak Vineyard
Caldwell Vineyard
Covert Estate
Di Costanzo
Farella Vineyards
Faust Winery
Favia
Italics Winegrowers
Le Chanceux
Palmaz Vineyards
PATEL Napa Valley
Rocca Family Vineyards
Scalon Cellars
Sciandri Family Vineyards
Shadybrook Estate
Silver Stag Winery
Sodaro Estate Wines
Tulocay Winery

The wine industry is dynamic. For up-to-date listings, please visit individual AVA websites.

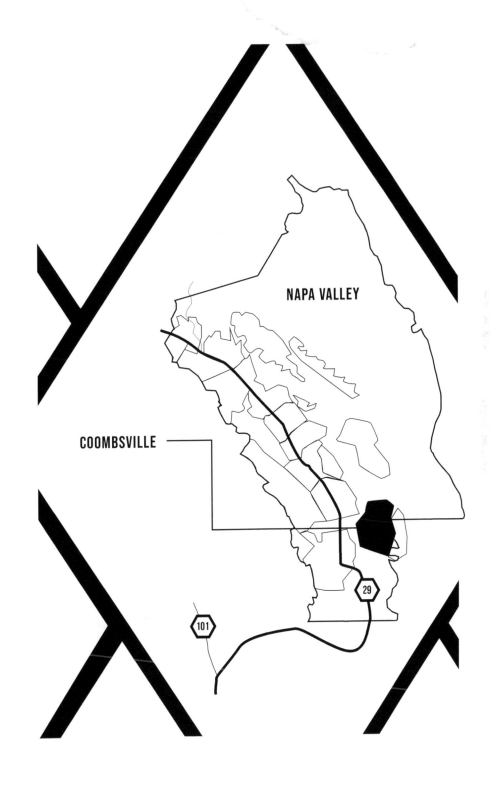

ABOU-

COOMBSVILLE

ITALICS WINE-GROWERS

TAYLOR MARTIN

MANAGING PARTNER

WHAT DO YOU LIKE MOST ABOUT COOMBSVILLE?

Coombsville encompasses a volcanic caldera, created by a violent volcanic explosion several million years ago. Influenced by the cool air that moves in off San Pablo Bay six miles to the west, the landscape holds countless micro-climates and landscapes that move and hold air in unique ways. For example, the Italics Winegrowers vineyard covers just over 30 acres and the temperature difference between the two most extreme aspects can exceed 20 degrees on any given day.

The community also has an inescapable quaintness about it. The terroir has historically presented extreme challenges to grape farmers, so most landowners grazed horses instead. Over time, the large horse ranches were split up and the community of Coombsville began to take shape. Less than 11 percent of the AVA's acres are planted in grapevines, giving the area a unique, rustic and inviting feel.

▼

WHAT EFFECT DOES YOUR REGION HAVE ON THE GRAPES THAT GROW HERE?

Coombsville has only recently come into its own as a winegrowing region for a variety of reasons. More than 900 feet of compressed volcanic ash separate the vines from the domestic water table, making commercially sustainable viticulture a venture rife with logistical challenges. Water quality management and conservation are ever-present talking points at community meetings. Many vintners plumb recycled water to their properties.

Additionally, unique inversion layers create air flow patterns that drastically impact the growing conditions as vines can experience shifts in temperature of over 50 degrees from daytime highs to nighttime lows. Add to that the 20-knot winds that blow through the rows every afternoon and you've got a region famous for producing bold and beautiful wines. All these challenges lead to more attention being paid to the vines, and that leads to a unique expression of the individual varieties.

WHAT WILL WE NOTICE WHEN TASTING A WINE FROM YOUR AVA?

Coombsville's terroir produces complex, dark, and beautiful red wines. While there are a few outstanding Chardonnay vineyards spread around the area,

Bordeaux varieties dominate the landscape along with a few intermittent Syrah vineyards. Dark red and black fruits dominate the palate, with layered complexity that accentuates the luscious juiciness and tannin structure.

WHAT DO PEOPLE MISUNDERSTAND ABOUT YOUR AVA?

People are more likely to overlook Coombsville than misunderstand it. It's only been officially designated as an AVA since 2012, so consumers are just now being introduced to the area as the Coombsville sub-AVA of Napa Valley. This area doesn't have the density of wineries or vineyards that other AVAs have, nor the overall number of wineries. There are only around 20 places you can even visit, so it truly is a hidden gem.

WHAT DO YOU WANT PEOPLE TO KNOW ABOUT YOUR AVA?

While Coombsville is a newcomer to the ranks of approved AVAs in Napa Valley, the fruit has been making an impact since the 1970s. Winemakers have held their vineyard sources in Coombsville close to the chest and utilized the wine as a valuable ace in the hole at the blending table. Now that the secret is out, the draw of Coombsville vineyards is growing at a rapid pace.

 AVA 2

COOMBSVILLE

DRIVE THROUGH NAPA

CLIMATE

Weather is moderated by its proximity to
San Pablo Bay. Daily average high temperatures
can be as much as 10 degrees cooler during the hot
months than most other AVAs, and heat spikes tend
to be less severe.

ELEVATION

100 to 1,000 feet.

RAINFALL

25 inches annually.

SOILS

Primarily weathered volcanic rock and alluvial
deposits from the Vaca Range that surrounds
the region.

PRINCIPAL VARIETIES

Dominated by Cabernet Sauvignon on the
hillsides with Merlot, Chardonnay, Syrah
and Pinot Noir in the lower, cooler sites.

▼

Nestled in a small foothill valley south of Atlas Peak, and just a 10-minute drive east of the city of Napa, Coombsville has long produced sought-after grapes. Named for Nathan Coombs, who founded the city of Napa in 1848,

COOMBSVILLE BENEFITS FROM CONSISTENCY OF SOIL, CLIMATE AND TERROIR.

In that regard it has the least variety of any of Napa's nested appellations. It rises from almost sea level at the edge of the Napa River on its western border to about 1,900 feet, the top of the Vaca Mountains. That source provides the predominantly volcanic soil in much of the area.

Because of its proximity to San Pablo Bay, this AVA remains cool year-round, although the warmest and highest hillside vineyards produce fine Cabernet Sauvignon and other Bordeaux grapes.

In cooler spots you'll find

CHARDONNAY
PINOT NOIR
SYRAH

Most of its 40 or so vineyards are between 100 and 500 feet above sea level, although a few are located at above 1,000 feet. Because its climate is prevailingly moderate, with no frosts and few scorchingly hot days, Coombsville is known for its long hang time. Conditions are ideal for slow ripening.

One of Napa's newer appellations (it was designated in 2011), this 11,000-acre region was once known as the "low-rent area" of the valley. For years it was more valued as pasture land than as a site for viticulture, considered too cool for quality grape growing. But that attitude has changed in the last few years.

NOW THERE ARE ALMOST 1,400 ACRES OF VINEYARDS PLANTED PRINCIPALLY TO CABERNET SAUVIGNON AND OTHER BORDEAUX GRAPES, AS WELL AS SYRAH AND CHARDONNAY.

Phelps Insignia, Viader, Merus, Paul Hobbs, Pahlmeyer, Dunn, Quintessa and other quality wineries buy Coombsville grapes. John Caldwell and Andy Erickson are probably the area's most renowned winemakers.

—

PRICE TO RATING CHART

THE GRAPH INDICATES VIVINO USERS'
AVERAGE RATINGS FOR WINES AT
DIFFERENT PRICE POINTS IN
THIS AVA.

DATA POWERED BY VIVINO

COOMBSVILLE

PRICE TO RATING CHART

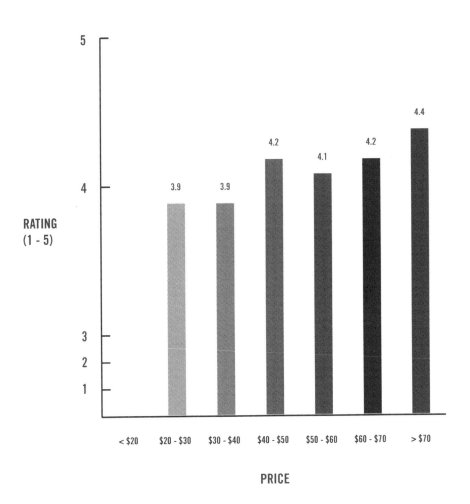

RATING
(1 - 5)

PRICE

SOUTH TO NORTH

AVA 3:

WILD HORSE VALLEY

WILD HORSE VALLEY

WINERIES & VINEYARDS

Olivia Brion

The wine industry is dynamic. For up-to-date listings, please visit individual AVA websites.

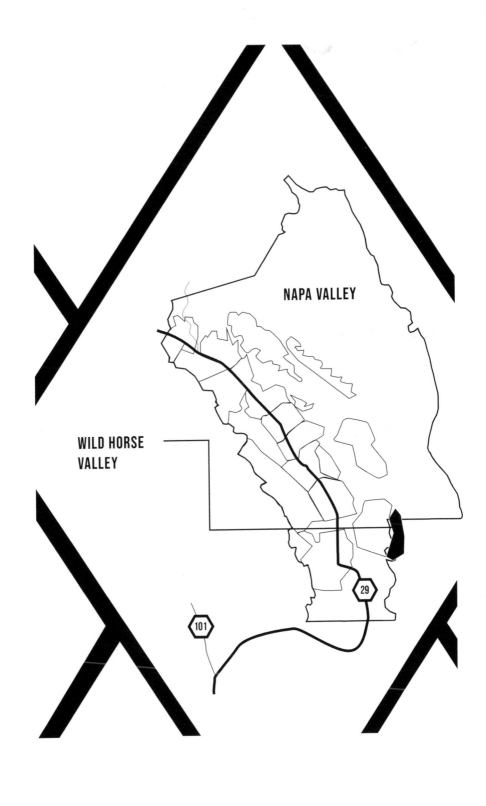

 AVA 3

WILD HORSE VALLEY

DRIVE THROUGH NAPA

CLIMATE

Due to its elevation and proximity to San Pablo Bay, part of Wild Horse Valley is the coolest spot in all the Napa Valley AVAs, although its eastern reaches are warmer because of their greater distance from the water. The air mass that passes over Carneros cools another 10 degrees by the time it rises to the elevation of this AVA.

ELEVATION

850 to 2,130 feet.

RAINFALL

35 inches annually.

SOILS

Volcanic in origin, with basaltic red color; shallow with limited water retention, so irrigation is often essential.

PRINCIPAL VARIETIES & CHARACTERISTICS

Pinot Noir: Bright berry and cherry fruit with great acidity. Chardonnay: Crisp, floral, aromatic, with distinctive pear-mineral flavors and bright acidity.

▼

Wild Horse Valley's borders overlap Napa and Solano counties, making it a bit of an outlier. Located in the Vaca Mountains, it is one of the cooler AVAs in Napa, although its far-south location translates into more hours of sunshine than most other areas of the valley. The cooling effect of nearby San Pablo Bay means that this area is ideal for Pinot Noir. Chardonnay is also planted here.

The AVA is one of the smallest in the country, covering only 3,300 acres of land in the hills above Coombsville. Wild Horse Valley is elevated well above the Silverado Trail – the valley floor rises to roughly 1,400 feet above sea level. This altitude raises the vines above the fog line, but the valley's western slopes are open to chilly marine breezes. Intense sunshine, high diurnal temperature variation and those reliable breezes result in healthy vineyards capable of producing ripe, intensely colored wines that are balanced in both acidity and tannins.

THE LEAN MOUNTAIN SOILS IN WILD HORSE VALLEY STRESS THE VINES, SO THEY'RE FORCED TO BURROW AND DEVELOP COMPLEX, HEALTHY ROOT SYSTEMS AS THEY SEARCH FOR WATER AND NUTRIENTS. AT HARVEST, ALL THIS STRESS HELPS REDUCE YIELDS AND INCREASES THE INTENSITY OF THE FRUIT.

In fact, Wild Horse Valley's soils are too much of a bad thing: smaller producers can operate profitably, but large-scale producers can't develop cost-effective vineyards.

TODAY, THERE ARE ONLY AROUND 100 CULTIVATED ACRES, AND ONLY A FEW ARTISANAL PRODUCERS ARE ACTIVE THERE.

Wild Horse Valley's first vineyards were planted in the late 19th century, and it was one of the first AVAs to be established in Napa, although it was never a major source of wine grapes. The winegrowing zone straddles the county line between Napa and its eastern neighbor Solano County; only wines grown in the Napa portion of Wild Horse Valley can claim the better-known and more lucrative Napa Valley title.

Wild Horse Valley sustained heavy damage in the 2017 wildfires.

SOUTH TO NORTH

AVA 4:

MOUNT VEEDER

▼

MOUNT VEEDER
WINERIES & VINEYARDS

Alpha Omega
Angelo Cellars
Anthem Winery & Vineyards
Beringer
Boich Family Cellar
Brandlin
Brioso Vineyard
Bruadair Vineyard
Chamboulé Winery
Darioush
Domaine Chandon
Fohr Vineyards
Fontanella Family Winery
Foyt Family Wines
Gamble Family Vineyards
Godspeed Vineyards
HALL Wines
Hensley Family Vineyards
Hess Collection
Kukeri Wines
Lagier Meredith
Lampyridae Vineyards
Lokoya
Marketta Winery
Mayacamas Vineyards
Mithra Winery
Mount Veeder Magic Vineyards
Mount Veeder Winery
Mt. Brave
Nosotros Vineyards
Paratus Vineyards
Peter Franus Wine Company
Pilcrow
Progeny
Pulido-Walker Estate Vineyard
Random Ridge Winery
Robert Craig Winery

Sky Vineyards
Thomas-Hsi Vineyards
Trinchero Family Estates
VGS Chateau Potelle
Vinoce Vineyards
WaterMark
Wing Canyon Vineyard
Yates Family Vineyard

The wine industry is dynamic. For up-to-date listings, please visit individual AVA websites.

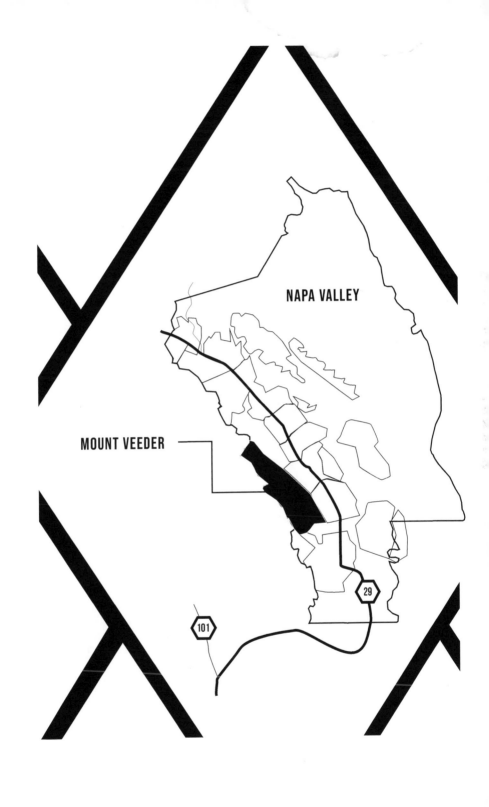

NAPA-1

MOUNT VEEDER

THE HESS COLLECTION

DAVE GUFFY

DIRECTOR OF WINEMAKING

WHAT DO YOU LIKE MOST ABOUT MOUNT VEEDER?

I like the fact that Mount Veeder is one of the smallest appellations in Napa, but it has a reputation for making big Cabernets. I'm talking small in terms of the tonnage that comes out of Mount Veeder; only 1 percent of Napa grapes come from there. The weird thing is that it's the largest AVA in Napa at 25 square miles. The reason for that discrepancy is that so much of Mount Veeder is still wild. It's largely thick forest surrounding these little vineyards that were carved out of the hillside many years ago.

WHAT EFFECT DOES THE MOUNT VEEDER AVA HAVE ON THE GRAPES THAT YOU GROW HERE?

Mount Veeder is like every other mountain appellation in most respects. On the valley floor there's lots of soil depth. On Mount Veeder our soil depth is 10 to 20 inches over shale, hardpan or big boulders. That results in small vines, which always always create bigger wines. Berry size is much smaller. You get a bigger tannin profile. We use Malbec in our Bordeaux blends. It tends to grow really well in cooler climates like ours. It brings a beautifully full mid-palate weight to the wine without any astringent tannin.

▼

DESCRIBE THE TERROIR OF YOUR REGION. WHAT WILL WE NOTICE WHEN TASTING A WINE FROM MOUNT VEEDER?

Mount Veeder has a long and cool growing season. The soils are volcanic and rocky, so the vines yield small berries. Yet the best Cabernets show elegance and restraint with full structure and good acidity, setting up excellent ageability. Mount Veeder wine has dark fruit characteristics, like many mountain reds.

WHAT DO PEOPLE MISUNDERSTAND ABOUT YOUR AVA ?

That we are too far off Highway 29 to come visit. The Hess Collection is just a brief 15-minute scenic drive up Redwood Road.

WHAT ELSE DO YOU WANT PEOPLE TO KNOW ABOUT YOUR AVA?

Mount Veeder is a place for nature lovers. We're not on the way to anywhere, and it's a windy road that gets down to one lane on the way to Sonoma. But one of my favorite things about this place is that it's still a mountain. It's more about the rugged landscape and the forest than the vineyards. You have to really respect that; it makes us special. We don't have many neighboring vineyards. We have about 300 acres combined in three different vineyards that are plantable. And we have 600 acres that are just forest and open land. And that is the way it will stay, for good reason. The biodiversity in the forest has the right combination of bugs to keep things in balance in the vineyard. At Hess, we've never sprayed insecticide in the vineyards. We're sustainable all the way.

All our vineyards are above the fog line, so the sun is constant. But most people up here harvest later than on the valley floor because it's so much cooler. And the older vines here tend to root so deeply that we sometimes don't irrigate them. We get 45 to 50 inches of rain here in a typical year, occasionally a lot more. So we don't have to use much water.

 AVA 4

MOUNT VEEDER

DRIVE THROUGH NAPA

CLIMATE

Cool to moderate, with most vineyards above the fog line, meaning warmer nights and cooler days than the valley floor. Typical mid-summer high temperatures are about 85 degrees.

ELEVATION

500 to 2,600 feet.

RAINFALL

35 inches annually.

SOILS

Sedimentary based, former seabed, shallow and generally well drained, as well as quite acidic, with low fertility. Most have a sandy or sandy-loam texture.

PRINCIPAL VARIETIES & CHARACTERISTICS

Ageability is a hallmark of Mount Veeder wines. Cabernet Sauvignon, Merlot, Zinfandel: Low yields give red wines a firm, tannic structure with strong, earthy berry aromas and rich, powerful flavors. Chardonnay: mineral-ish, apple-y, some citrus flavors, with good acidity.

▼

Mount Veeder was named for the Dutch Presbyterian pastor, Peter Veeder, who lived in Napa during the years around the Civil War and loved to hike frequently on the mountain. Winemaking on Mount Veeder began in 1864. Captain Stelham Wing uncorked the first Mount Veeder vintage at the Napa County Fair with a wine hailing from what is now Wing Canyon Vineyard.

The German influence continued into the 1880s. Streich Winery (now Yates Family Vineyard) was founded by Ernest Streich, and the Fisher Winery (now Mayacamas Vineyards) was built by John Henry Fisher of Stuttgart.

In 1900, Theodore Geir, a flamboyant German-born Oakland liquor dealer, bought the property that would later become the Christian Brothers' Mont La Salle Winery and, later still, the Hess Collection Winery. Early in the 20th century there were 20 vineyards and six wineries on the slopes of Mount Veeder.

Prohibition decimated the vineyards, and they came back slowly: Mayacamas Vineyards in 1951 and Bernstein Vineyards in 1964.

During the 1960s Mount Veeder became a haven for "back to the earth" types. Among them were Arlene and Michael Bernstein, whose 1973 Cabernet Sauvignon was the first wine to bear the Mount Veeder designation on its label.

The wines of Mount Veeder share the attributes of the vintners that grow them: a deeply expressive character and great diversity.

THE GRAPES' DISTINCTIVE PROFILE IS FORMED BY THE FAMOUS MOUNT VEEDER TERROIR: FIRM STRUCTURE, ROBUST SPICE AND RICH FRUIT FLAVORS THAT HOLD WITH AGE.

Mount Veeder reds can be floridly spiced and intensely flowery, with hints of brambleberry and minerality. White wines share a mineral edge that is softened by rich stone fruit lusciousness, often with a hint of citrus.

CABERNET SAUVIGNON, CHARDONNAY AND SYRAH PREDOMINATE ON MOUNT VEEDER.

However, there are at least 18 varieties grown on the mountain, including uncommon plantings such as Carignan and Mataro.

▼

—

PRICE TO RATING CHART

THE GRAPH INDICATES VIVINO USERS'
AVERAGE RATINGS FOR WINES AT
DIFFERENT PRICE POINTS IN
THIS AVA.

DATA POWERED BY VIVINO

MOUNT VEEDER

PRICE TO RATING CHART

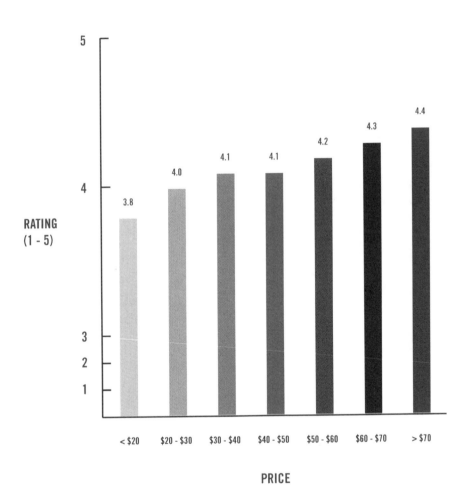

RATING
(1 - 5)

PRICE

SOUTH TO NORTH

AVA 5:

OAK KNOLL

ŌAK KNOLL
WINERIES & VINEYARDS

Andre Vineyard
Anthony August Vineyard
Big Ranch Vineyards
Black Stallion Estate Winery
Boyd Family Vineyards
Celani Family Vineyards
Corley Family Napa Valley
Cunat Family Vineyards
Darms Lane
Eleven Eleven
FARM Napa Valley
Fortunati Vineyards
Ideology Cellars
Okapi
Kasten Family Vineyards
Kelly Family Vineyards
Laird Family Estate
Lamoreaux Vineyards | Oak Knoll Ranch
Las Trancas Vineyard
Materra | Cunat Family Vineyards
Matthiasson Winery
Medero Vineyards – Coq en Fer
Monticello Vineyards
O'Brien Estate
Padis Vineyards
Robert Biale Vineyards
Silenus Winery
Steelemack Wines
Trefethen Family Vineyards

The wine industry is dynamic. For up-to-date listings, please visit individual AVA websites.

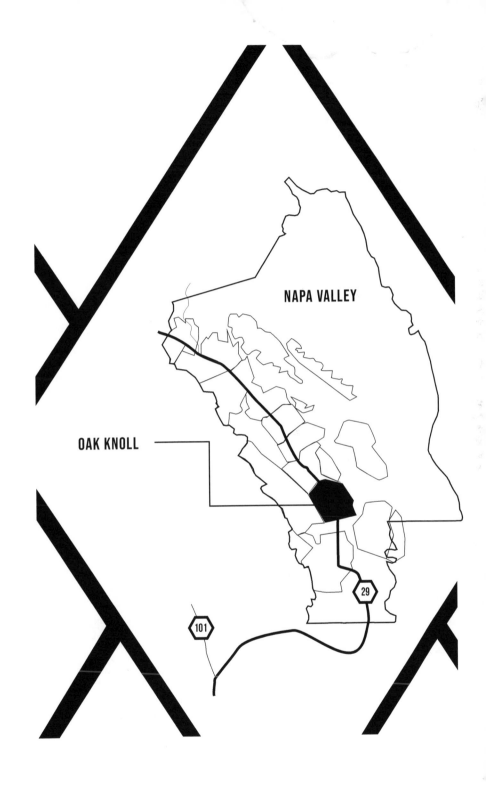

NAPA VALLEY

OAK KNOLL

101

29

▼

OAK KNOLL

TREFETHEN FAMILY VINEYARDS

LORENZO TREFETHEN

THIRD GENERATION VINTNER

WHAT DO YOU LIKE MOST ABOUT OAK KNOLL?

The fog. I adore the fog. It's like a built-in air conditioner, keeping both the vines and the people in the Oak Knoll District at just the right temperature.

Every evening, cool marine air from the Pacific blows in through the Golden Gate, up the San Francisco Bay, and into Napa Valley. Its effect is strong in the Oak Knoll District, where no matter how sunny and warm the afternoon is, every evening is sweater weather, even in midsummer. The grapes love this, and so do I – I sleep with my windows open every night in a nice, cool room. The fog sticks around in the morning, keeping us cool until it burns off, moderating the rise in temperature that happens in the afternoon before returning in the evening to renew its embrace.

WHAT EFFECT DOES YOUR REGION HAVE ON THE GRAPES THAT GROW HERE?

The Oak Knoll District is the most diverse sub-AVA in Napa. We grow an incredible number of grapes here – around 20 different varieties at last count.

▼

The mild, marine-influenced climate of the Oak Knoll District creates the longest growing season in Napa Valley. Our soils warm up early in springtime, giving us an early start, while the fog keeps us cool in the summer. This gentle climate allows for slow, even ripening, and most vintages are capped with a beautiful warm fall that pushes the last of the grapes to maturity. As a result, it is one of very few places in the world where early-ripening varieties, like Chardonnay, and late-ripening varieties, like Cabernet Sauvignon, both thrive. Not too cold, not too hot – the Oak Knoll District is Napa's sweet spot.

WHAT WILL WE NOTICE WHEN TASTING A WINE FROM OAK KNOLL?

Many up-valley wineries source fruit from the Oak Knoll District to bring a certain freshness to their blends.

As a result of the cooling influence of our beloved fog, wines from the Oak Knoll District tend to exhibit a mouthwatering acidity and levity in their fruit, contributing to a liveliness on the palate. Our mild climate also moderates the development of tannins and sugar, generally leading to elegant, balanced, graceful wines with relatively low alcohol levels that age beautifully in the cellar. As the wines soften over time, that brightness still shines through.

WHAT DO PEOPLE MISUNDERSTAND ABOUT YOUR AVA?

Because it was established in 2004, people think the Oak Knoll District is new, but wine grapes have been here for a very long time. In 1852, Captain Joseph W. Osborne, founder of Oak Knoll Ranch, planted some of the first European grape varieties in California. His work in the vineyards, along with Agoston Haraszthy of Sonoma, marked him as one of the fathers of the California fine wine industry.

Today, the Oak Knoll District continues to define itself with its vineyards. There are more individual growers here than in any other Napa AVA, and some of the wineries based here are fully estate, meaning they only make wine from the grapes they grow themselves. Oak Knoll District fruit has also long been a part of many iconic Napa wines that draw from multiple appellations, including those by Joseph Phelps, Heitz, and Caymus.

WHAT ELSE DO YOU WANT PEOPLE TO KNOW ABOUT YOUR AVA?

That the Oak Knoll District is a delicious place to be! The combination of quality and diversity in the Oak Knoll District is hard to beat, in our vineyards and also in our gardens. Alongside all the celebrated wines made from our grapes, our local produce features in many of Napa's famed restaurants. If you're lucky enough to dine at The French Laundry, for example, you'll probably enjoy some vegetables that Thomas Keller's team grows in their garden here at Trefethen. And again, the diversity of what grows well in this AVA is extraordinary. In our own gardens, which we share with our employees, we grow both apples and oranges. If you're a farmer, the Oak Knoll District truly feels like paradise.

115

 AVA 5

OAK KNOLL

DRIVE THROUGH NAPA

CLIMATE

Moderate to cool. Marine air and fog can remain until late morning. Late afternoon breezes frequently occur, maintaining slightly cooler temperatures than the upper valley. Mid-summer temperatures may reach 92 degrees and drop to around 50 at night.

ELEVATION

Sea level to 800 feet.

RAINFALL

36 inches annually.

SOILS

Formed by Dry Creek, the valley's largest alluvial fan is the defining feature of the district. The northwest area is composed of volcanically based soils with stony or gravelly consistency. In the south and east the soil transitions to gravel and silty clay loam.

PRINCIPAL VARIETIES & CHARACTERISTICS

Cabernet Sauvignon, Chardonnay, Merlot, Pinot Noir, Sauvignon Blanc and Syrah. Merlot and Cabernet Sauvignon are well suited to a longer growing season with slightly cooler temperatures and significant hang time. Dominant flavors in the reds: Bordeaux-like hints of cassis, tobacco and spice. Chardonnay: crisp apple, tropical fruit, gentle minerality. Reds and whites alike show an elegance borne of balance.

117

▼

The Oak Knoll District is one of Napa Valley's oldest grape-growing areas. Vines were first planted here around 1851.

Captain Joseph W. Osborne came to California in 1850 during the boom years of the Gold Rush. In 1851 he secured a significant piece of prime farmland three miles south of Yountville. Osborne named his property Oak Knoll.

Osborne dived into winemaking at Oak Knoll. He introduced some of the first desirable European grape varieties to the Golden State, transporting many varieties of European grapes from Massachusetts.

Oak Knoll was designated the state's best farm by the California Agricultural Society in 1856, spurring more growth. By the late 1850s Osborne's 50-acre vineyard was easily the largest and most successful in all of Napa Valley. Only his untimely murder in 1863 by a former employee kept Osborne from becoming a bigger name in California's wine industry.

The next generation brought more refinement. Eshcol Ranch vineyard was planted near Oak Knoll in the early 1880s. Eshcol is remembered for its meticulously maintained vineyards as well as a gravity-flow winery designed and built in 1886 by pioneering winery architect Hamden McIntyre, who also designed Inglenook, Greystone and Far Niente. Eshcol Ranch was a leading producer of award-winning California wine throughout the 1880s.

Phylloxera, Prohibition and changing tastes altered the region. By the mid-1960s, Oak Knoll's vineyards were largely gone. Walnuts and hay were the principal source of farming income.

▼

Its fortunes changed in the next decade. Grapes from the district's vineyards were in the top-ranked Chardonnay wine of the 1976 Judgment of Paris and Gault Millau Magazine's World Wine Olympics. In the 1980s, Oak Knoll red varieties, especially its Cabernets, swept many categories at statewide competitions.

The Oak Knoll District of Napa Valley became an AVA in 2004, and about half of the district's 8,300 acres are under vine. It has the most grapevines of any wholly contained appellation of the Napa Valley. It is located north of the City of Napa and south of Yountville. Mt. Veeder is the western border and the Silverado Trail defines its eastern boundary. Some of Napa Valley's iconic wineries have made their reputations with Oak Knoll District fruit.

Oak Knoll lies at the southern end of Napa Valley where the growing season is longer—cooler in summer than the warmer Upper Valley and drier in winter. The marine influence from San Pablo Bay is strong here, with foggy mornings and cool summer nights. Summer daytime temperatures can average 10 degrees cooler than St. Helena, creating the longest growing season in the valley. Cool nights and slowly rising daytime temperatures allow a naturally long hang time for fruit.

This even warming and cooling creates a happy medium where it's warm enough to perfectly ripen red varieties like Cabernet Sauvignon, Merlot, Malbec, Petit Verdot, and Zinfandel while cool enough for grapes like Chardonnay and Pinot Noir.

▼

—

PRICE TO RATING CHART

THE GRAPH INDICATES VIVINO USERS'
AVERAGE RATINGS FOR WINES AT
DIFFERENT PRICE POINTS IN
THIS AVA.

DATA POWERED BY VIVINO

OAK KNOLL

PRICE TO RATING CHART

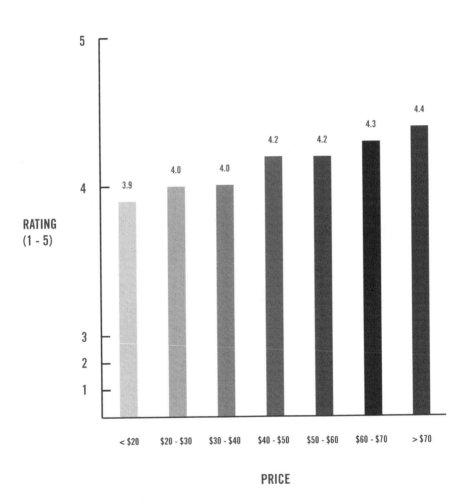

RATING
(1 - 5)

PRICE

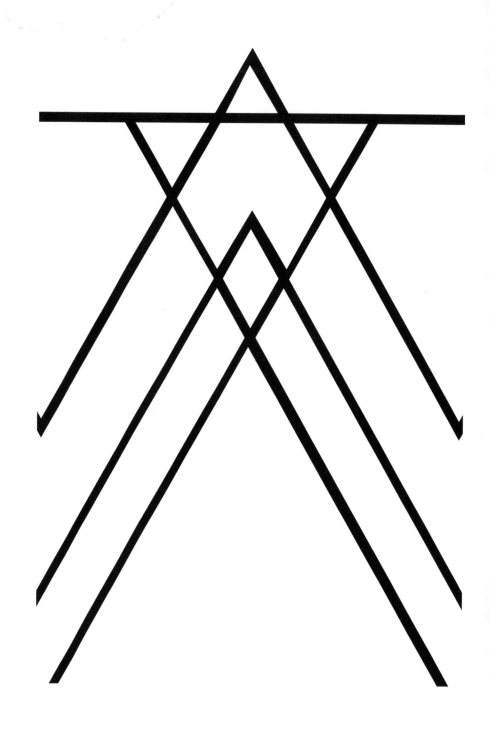

SOUTH TO NORTH

AVA 6:

YOUNTVILLE

▼

YOUNTVILLE
WINERIES & VINEYARDS

Abigail Adams WInes
Ad Vivum
Beau Vigne
Bell Wine Cellars
Blankiet Estate
Casa Piena
Chanticleer Estate Wines
Clif Lede Vineyards
Corley Family
Domaine Chandon
Dominus Estate
Elyse Winery
Gemstone Vineyards
Gentleman Farmer Wines
Goosecross Cellars
Grand Wines Napa
Herb Lamb Vineyards
Hestan Vineyards
Hill Family Estate
Hoopes Vineyard
Hope & Grace
Hopper Creek Vineyard
J Gregory Wines
JCB Tasting Salon
Jessup Cellars
Kale Wines
Kapcsandy Family Winery
Keever Vineyards
Paraduxx Winery
Perata Vineyards
Pina Cellars
Rocca Family
Steltzner Vineyards
Stewart Cellars
Switchback Ridge
Tom Scott Vineyards

The wine industry is dynamic. For up-to-date listings, please visit individual AVA websites.

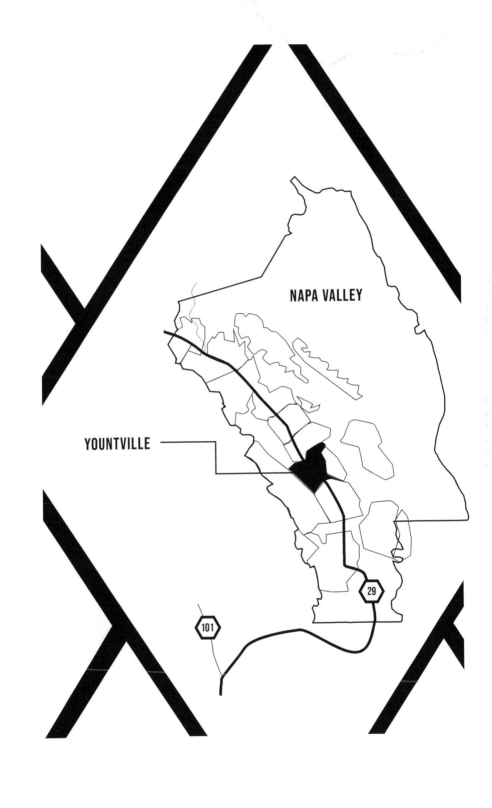

NAPA VALLEY

YOUNTVILLE

101

29

YOUNTVILLE

KEEVER VINEYARDS

CELIA WELCH

WINEMAKER

WHAT DO YOU LIKE MOST ABOUT YOUNTVILLE?

I love the diversity of the AVA. I work with the fruit on the westernmost edges of Yountville, which are steep, rocky slopes that yield small crops of very dark Cabernet with lovely ripe tannins, but we also see fantastic Sauvignon Blanc, Merlot and other varieties being grown east of Yountville, closer to the Napa River.

WHAT EFFECT DOES THE REGION HAVE ON THE GRAPES THAT ARE GROWN THERE?

With a diversity of soils, the region gives us quite diverse wine styles. The one constant throughout the AVA is the cooling breezes, which pick up at around 3 p.m. on most summer afternoons. They cool the fruit nicely, protecting it from the highest temperatures that vineyards farther up-valley might experience.

WHAT CHARACTERISTICS WILL WE NOTICE WHEN TASTING A WINE FROM YOUR AVA?

Although quality is exceptional throughout Yountville's vineyards, you'll see individual influences from specific places within the AVA (which soils, which exposure, east-facing vineyards as compared to valley floor vineyards, etc.). One common trait would be the natural balance of tannins and acidity in these wines, because of the moderating influence of nearby San Pablo Bay.

WHAT MIGHT PEOPLE MISUNDERSTAND ABOUT YOUR AVA?

When many people hear the word "Yountville," they immediately associate the word with world-class dining, hotels, and spa experiences. Sometimes they don't realize that many of their favorite wines are also grown and produced in Yountville.

WHAT ELSE DO YOU WANT PEOPLE TO KNOW ABOUT YOUNTVILLE?

Yountville AVA encompasses great vineyards and wineries, a charming community, the country's largest veterans home, the Napa Valley Museum, an ecological reserve area next to the Napa River, and Napa's history going back to George Yount, who planted the first European grapevines in Napa Valley. The climate, which has led to worldwide acclaim for Yountville's farm-to-table restaurants, also explains why the wines of Yountville are consistently rated among the best in the world.

 AVA 6

YOUNTVILLE

DRIVE THROUGH NAPA

CLIMATE

Moderate, with marine influence and fog contributing to cool summer mornings and the strong breezes of San Pablo Bay keeping afternoons more comfortable than farther up the valley. Mid-summer peak temperatures may reach the low 90s, with hefty diurnal dips down to the mid-50s.

ELEVATION

20 to 200 feet.

RAINFALL

32 inches annually.

SOILS

Principally gravelly silt loams, sedimentary in origin, and gravelly alluvial soils with rock; moderately fertile.

PRINCIPAL VARIETIES & CHARACTERISTICS

Cabernet Sauvignon, Merlot: Yountville favors Cabernet and Merlot with ripe, violet aromas, rich but supple flavors, and firm tannins.

▼

Yountville enjoys an enviable location in the very heart of the Napa Valley, halfway between the northern shores of San Pablo Bay and the southern slopes of Mount St. Helena, and it's a respected producer of Cabernet Sauvignon and Merlot. Yountville's best wines are some of the most sought-after in California.

The AVA surrounds the town of Yountville, which lies mid-valley between the town of Napa and the village of St. Helena. Most of the vineyards can be found on the Napa Valley floor, although in the western part of the AVA vines are planted on rocky, undulating slopes in the foothills of the Mayacamas Mountains. Yountville is surrounded by some of Napa's most famous appellations. To the north lies Oakville, to the west Mount Veeder and to the east is Stags Leap.

Yountville is named after George C. Yount, a North Carolina-born trapper who travelled with William Wolfskill's party from New Mexico to California in 1831. Yount trapped sea otters on the Channel Islands before moving to Sonoma in 1834, where he found work as a carpenter for General Mariano Guadalupe Vallejo. Through the influence of Vallejo, Yount received the Rancho Caymus land grant in 1836 and became the first permanent settler in Napa Valley. Yount planted Napa's first non-mission vineyard at Rancho Caymus in 1836.

Yount's empire eventually took in what is now one of the most valuable stretches of wine-industry real estate in the country.

Rancho Caymus (the ancestor of Caymus Vineyard in Rutherford) covered the huge tract of land that is now part of Rutherford, Oakville and Yountville. A later acquisition, Rancho La Jota, was situated on the eastern slopes of Howell Mountain. La Jota winery was founded there in 1898.

Today, Yountville's obsession with Cabernet Sauvignon and Merlot is counterbalanced by small plantings of Syrah and Petite Sirah. The most popular white varieties are Sauvignon Blanc and Chardonnay.

Although the town of Yountville is one of Napa's warmer spots, its vineyards, located just to the east, regularly catch a bit of ocean influence, and they're noticeably cooler than town. That's because of an unusual topographical feature. Cool marine air currents from San Pablo Bay to the south are trapped when they reach what are known as the Yountville Mounts, even on the warmest summer days. As a result, the grapes here have time to develop more slowly, imparting unique flavor characteristics and a pervading sense of terroir. As a result, Yountville's red wines are elegant, with big but rounded tannins and deep concentration. They are known to age very well.

A few important wineries can be found in Yountville: Dominus Estate, Domaine Chandon, Blankiet Estate, Cliff Lede Vineyards and others. The area is also a gourmand's paradise. It's home to Thomas Keller's Bouchon Bistro and Ad Hoc restaurants, as well as his world-famous French Laundry.

▼

—

PRICE TO RATING CHART

THE GRAPH INDICATES VIVINO USERS'
AVERAGE RATINGS FOR WINES AT
DIFFERENT PRICE POINTS IN
THIS AVA.

DATA POWERED BY VIVINO

YOUNTVILLE

PRICE TO RATING CHART

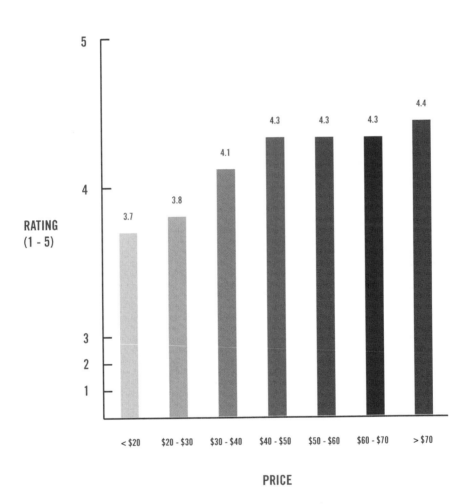

RATING
(1 - 5)

PRICE

SOUTH TO NORTH

AVA 7:

STAGS LEAP

▼

STAGS LEAP
WINERIES & VINEYARDS

Baldacci Family Vineyards
Cavus Vineyards
Chimney Rock Winery
Clos Du Val
Futo Vineyards
Husic Vineyards
Ilsley Vineyards
Lindstrom Wines
Lobo Wines
Malk Family Vineyards
Odette Estate
Pine Ridge Vineyards
Quixote Winery
Realm Cellars
Regusci Winery
Robert Sinskey Vineyards
Robinson Family Vineyards
Shafer Vineyards
Silverado Vineyards
Stag's Leap Wine Cellars
Stags Landing Vineyard
Stags' Leap Winery
Steltzner Vineyards
Taylor Family Vineyards

The wine industry is dynamic. For up-to-date listings, please visit individual AVA websites.

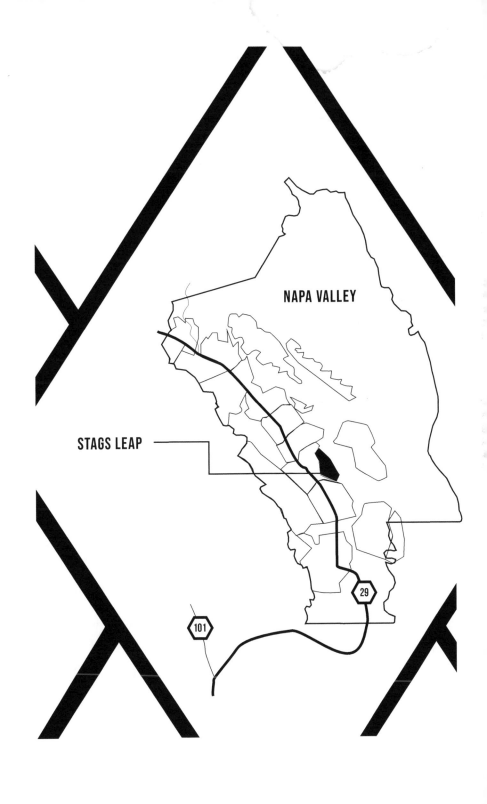

NAPA VALLEY

STAGS LEAP

29

101

STAGS LEAP

SILVERADO VINEYARDS

JON EMMERICH

WINEMAKER

WHAT DO YOU LIKE MOST ABOUT YOUR STAGS LEAP?

As a winemaker, the Stags Leap District AVA allows me to get our Cabernet Sauvignon grapes ripe (23 degrees Brix+) while still retaining good acidity and pH levels. This allows the wines to be fresh and lively without seeming under-ripe or green, or having to wait until the grapes turn to raisins to get flavor.

WHAT EFFECT DOES YOUR REGION HAVE ON THE GRAPES THAT GROW HERE?

The geography and soil give the Stags Leap District a unique quality that is not shared with many other AVAs. It is located in the east side of the Napa Valley, which is slightly drier in the warmer months of the growing season, and it is slightly cooler and foggier than the northern Napa AVAs. This part of the Stags Leap District looks like it is part of the valley floor, but in reality the soil is more gravelly loam than clay. It is composed of ancient volcanic material that was deposited from a massive landslide, so it is flat hillside soil, which drains perfectly.

WHAT WILL WE NOTICE WHEN TASTING A WINE FROM YOUR AVA?

What you will taste in a glass of Stags Leap District wine will be a fresh, bright wine with long, smooth tannins in the finish.

WHAT DO PEOPLE MISUNDERSTAND ABOUT YOUR AVA?

I believe that we need to move on from the "Judgment of Paris Tasting" historical perspective of the Stags Leap District region and talk about the new innovations in farming and winemaking that are making our wines even better. We are a generation removed from that time, and winemakers' knowledge of the area, and about winemaking in general, has grown a lot.

WHAT ELSE DO YOU WANT PEOPLE TO KNOW ABOUT YOUR STAGS LEAP?

I would like the consumer to know that Cabernet Sauvignon can be refreshing. Too often, Napa Cabernet is described in terms that make it seem overly heavy or unapproachable.

I would also like the consumer to know that the Stags Leap District AVA is the home of one of the three Napa Valley heritage Cabernet Sauvignon clones (UCD 30) and home to a host of wonderful family-owned wineries.

STAGS LEAP

DRIVE THROUGH NAPA

CLIMATE

Moderately warm, with afternoon marine winds cooling the warmer air radiating off the bare rocks of Stags Leap itself and the surrounding hillsides. Mid-summer temperatures can reach 100, but more regularly are in the mid-90s range.

ELEVATION

Sea level to 400 feet.

RAINFALL

30 inches annually.

SOILS

Volcanic gravel-loam on the floor of the valley, with rocky hillsides, and low to moderate fertility due to hard clay subsoils.

PRINCIPAL VARIETIES & CHARACTERISTICS

Cabernet Sauvignon, Merlot: Distinguished by lush, velvety textures, fine perfumed cherry and red berry flavors, supported by soft tannins. Sauvignon Blanc: Round and ripe, yet retains excellent citrus and apple flavors.

▼

Stags Leap District is one of Napa's most admired appellations. Cabernet Sauvignon takes on certain magical properties here, and it dominates the vineyards. Stags Leap Cabs are rich and deep, with ripe blackcurrant flavors, a zesty freshness and elegance, and well-structured but not overwhelming tannins.

Stags Leap is a small AVA only three miles long and a mile wide, located about five miles north of the Napa town site on the eastern side of the valley. It occupies a narrow strip of the valley floor, segregated slightly from the main valley by small north-south hills along its western boundary. At 2,700 acres, it's indeed tiny, but the land is precious. Stags Leap wineries occupy the majority of the AVA's space for vineyards, a pattern broken only by access roads and winery buildings.

Winemaking in the Stags Leap District began in the mid-19th century. In 1878, Tennessee native Terrill L. Grigsby built Occidental Winery, the first in the area (it's now Regusci Winery).

In 1893, San Francisco entrepreneur Horace Chase built the first winery associated with the name "Stags Leap." Where did it come from? One legend involves a stag that successfully eluded pursuing hunters by leaping to freedom across the region's picturesque peaks.

As with other parts of Napa, phylloxera and the effects of Prohibition decimated Stags Leap, and many vineyards were transformed into orchards to meet changing tastes and conditions.

In 1961, visionary grape grower Nathan Fay was the first to plant Cabernet Sauvignon vines in the Stags Leap District, which was considered too cool for that variety. Fay planted about 70 acres of Cabernet Sauvignon in coarse volcanic soil along the Silverado Trail.

At the time, there were only 800 acres of Cabernet Sauvignon planted in the entire country.

In the first harvest years, Fay sold most of his grapes to Joseph Heitz, and Heitz Cellar "Fay Vineyard" Cabernet Sauvignon was one of the first superstar Cabernets as as well as one of Napa's first vineyard-designated wines.

After the success of Heitz, Fay quickly found other buyers: Charles Krug Winery, Francis Mahoney of Carneros Creek Winery, and Robert Mondavi, as well as many home winemakers.

Of course, the most famous moment in Stags Leap history happened at the Judgment of Paris in 1976. A 1973 Stag's Leap Wine Cellars Cabernet Sauvignon beat French giants such as Château Mouton Rothschild and Château Haut-Brion. A decade later, the same wines were tasted head to head. This time, another Stags Leap wine took the gold: the 1972 Clos Du Val Cabernet Sauvignon.

Stags Leap's loose, porous soils force the Cabernet vines to grow strong, deep roots, which leads to more vigorous plants and higher-quality fruit. Climate is also crucial: only 15 miles from San Pablo Bay, Stags Leap is bathed regularly in cool, moist breezes. In summertime, fog is prevalent.

Cabernet Sauvignon makes up some 90 percent of the vineyards in Stags Leap District, although a small amount of Merlot is also grown, mostly for blending. Stags Leap is also responsible for creating tiny amounts of white wine – mostly oak-aged Chardonnay.

▼

—

PRICE TO RATING CHART

THE GRAPH INDICATES VIVINO USERS'
AVERAGE RATINGS FOR WINES AT
DIFFERENT PRICE POINTS IN
THIS AVA.

DATA POWERED BY VIVINO

STAGS LEAP

PRICE TO RATING CHART

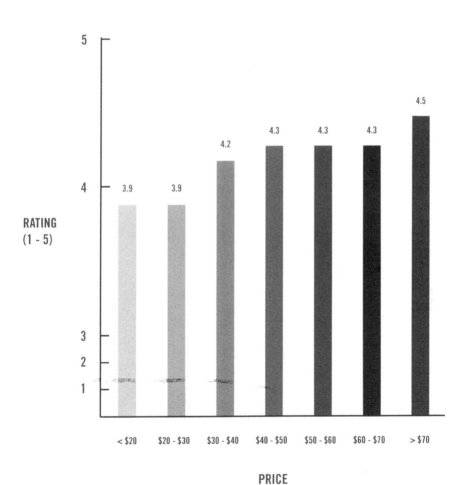

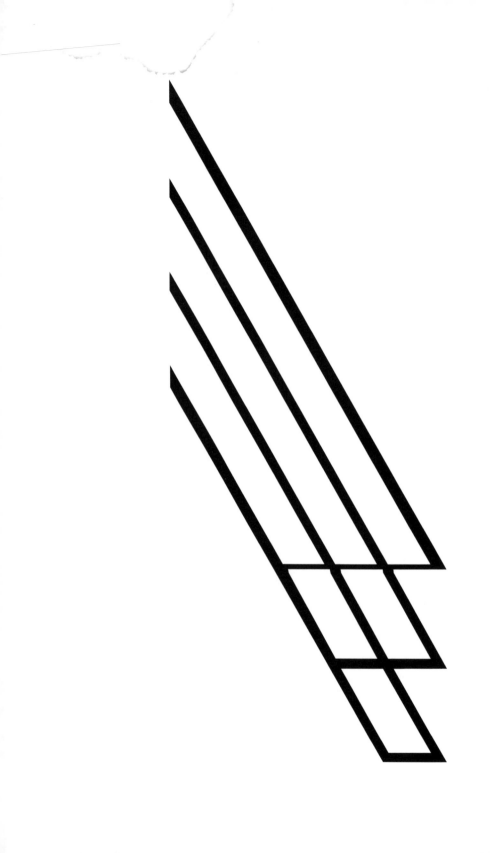

SOUTH TO NORTH

AVA 8:

ATLAS PEAK

▼

ATLAS PEAK
WINERIES & VINEYARDS

Acumen Wine
Aequitas Vineyards
Alpha Omega
ALTA Winery
Antica Napa Valley
Au Sommet
Bianchini Family Vineyard
Elan Vineyards
Guarachi Family Wines
HALL Wines
Hesperian Wines
Krupp Brothers Estates
Pahlmeyer
Prime Solum
Sill Family Vineyards
VinRoc

The wine industry is dynamic. For up-to-date listings, please visit individual AVA websites.

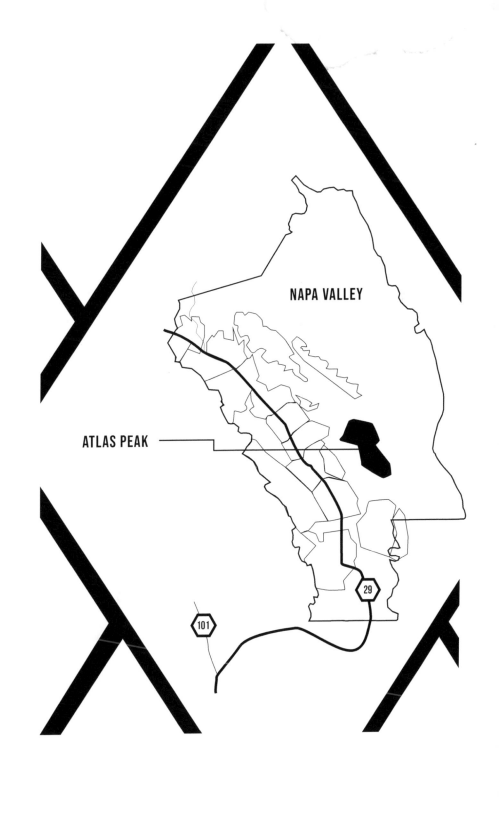

ATLAS PEAK

ALPHA OMEGA WINERY

JEAN HOEFLIGER

WINEMAKER

WHAT DO YOU LIKE MOST ABOUT ATLAS PEAK? WHAT EFFECT DOES THE AVA HAVE ON THE GRAPES THAT GROW HERE?

I like the fact that in an era of globalization, Atlas Peak has a distinct DNA. Big, dense and structured wines are the hallmarks of Atlas Peak. The elevation, the slope, the soil and the climate are all equally important.

Atlas Peak has fairly volcanic, rocky soil with good drainage. That means small berries. If you change the ratio of skin to juice you will have more concentrated wine.

Atlas Peak is not extremely hot. In a colder environment, you end up protecting the acidity a little better. Acidity is also an expression of tannins. You are left with wines with amazing depth and structure but with a tannic framework you have to closely manage. I like to say that acid is the backbone of the wine and the skeleton is the tannins.

On Atlas Peak you really have one thing to control: the skeleton. You must ripen the fruit to the right pH and acidity. The pH gives me a better indicator of the ripeness than sugar does. With warmer Napa AVAs, sugar rises very fast, but phenolic ripeness doesn't follow. Up there, the slower ripening mitigates that issue.

155

▼

WHAT WILL WE NOTICE WHEN TASTING A WINE FROM ATLAS PEAK?

We believe that a wine has to have a sense of place. One of the many reasons I like Atlas Peak is that the essence of this place is very clear in the wine. It's a fairly masculine wine overall because it's pretty big. The DNA is so distinct that people really enjoy it for that reason more than any other.

Alpha Omega wines from Atlas Peak are the definition of volcanic influence. Our high iron content soil makes for highly concentrated wines with a powerful tannic structure. You will notice more of an emphasis on dark fruit.

Atlas Peak generally has very poor, rocky soils with little water retention. You know you're going to stress the vine quite a bit. These vines have a high tolerance for extreme conditions.

One of the interesting stories of this AVA is that we really have two distinct regions. The grapes in those places develop differently and give two different profiles. We have a 25-year lease on a plateau between Atlas Peak and Pritchard Hill. It's almost like a different appellation: much earlier ripening, more topsoil, a little more of that fresh, fruit-driven profile.

The common thread for the AVA is definitely good acidity with a big tannic frame and dark fruit.

WHAT DO PEOPLE MISUNDERSTAND ABOUT YOUR AVA?

A common misperception about wines from Atlas Peak concerns their character. It is definitely possible to have finesse with tannic structure.

People remember us from a generation ago when there were large producers here making tannic wine. Now we are seeing fewer big producers with large acreages. Atlas Peak is supporting more and more smaller wineries with smaller tonnage (per acre) and more careful craft in the winemaking, coming closer to a true expression of the sense of place.

WHAT DO YOU WANT PEOPLE TO REMEMBER ABOUT YOUR AVA?

Atlas Peak is a unique appellation that mitigates the faults of Napa Valley. When the weather is too hot, the air circulation in Atlas Peak cools everything down. When it rains, the air movement and our excellent drainage solve any issue. And when the valley has fog, Atlas Peak does not because it sits above the fog line.

I think the days of instant gratification are over in the wine world. People are more interested in balance. And Atlas Peak wines have special advantages in being able to achieve that balance. I think of it as a tiny Napa of its own with just as much diversity, but fewer disadvantages.

ATLAS PEAK

DRIVE THROUGH NAPA

CLIMATE

Mountain-influenced, with temperatures about 10 to15 degrees cooler than the valley floor in summer. Large diurnal swing at lower elevations, but above the fog line there is a smaller day-to-night temperature variation, with summer temperatures rarely rising above 90 degrees.

ELEVATION

760 to 2,600 feet.

RAINFALL

38 inches annually.

SOILS

Volcanic in origin, with basaltic red color; shallow, with limited water retention, so irrigation is often essential.

PRINCIPAL VARIETIES & CHARACTERISTICS

Cabernet Sauvignon: Bright berry and cherry fruit, with more acidity than wines from Stags Leap District. Chardonnay: Crisp, floral, aromatic, with distinctive pear and mineral flavors and bright acidity.

Grape growing began around 1870 in this rugged district a few miles northeast of the city of Napa and directly east of Yountville. Zinfandel once thrived here, but Bordeaux varieties have largely taken its place.

During Prohibition and for many years afterward, the Atlas Peak area was used mainly by the dairy, cattle and lumber industries. In the mid-1980s, Atlas Peak Winery was born then quickly sold to a European conglomerate that included Allied Domecq Wines and Marchese Antinori. Its European owners developed it as a producer of Super Tuscan wines, especially Sangiovese. Now the rocky volcanic soil at Atlas Peak is home principally to Bordeaux varieties.

Atlas Peak was designated an AVA in 1992, and it's named after its highest point. (Atlas Peak is only 2,661 feet, not exactly Everest-like.) Its vineyards lie at a higher average elevation than most other districts in Napa, and they're approachable by two roads snaking up from the valley floor, Atlas Peak Road and Soda Canyon Road.

The vineyards' high perch means that the fog of the Pacific Ocean only lightly affects the grapes here.

Atlas Peak's 1,500 acres of vineyards are angled generally westward, allowing them to receive more sunlight than valley floor vineyards. The soil is usually rocky, porous and volcanic, with traces of red basalt. Its volcanic content allows air to permeate, and it heats and cools relatively quickly as a result. Atlas Peak's generally cool climate results in a longer growing season, longer hang time for the grapes, and less vine vigor – excellent conditions for growing premium Bordeaux grapes.

Though only about 14 wineries make their home in Atlas Peak, it's a popular source of grapes for other wineries.

MORE THAN 80 WINERIES IN THE NAPA VALLEY ALONE SOURCE FROM HERE.

Atlas Peak grapes are valued for their balanced acidity, and it's a district made for robust reds:

CABERNET SAUVIGNON
CABERNET FRANC
MALBEC
PETIT VERDOT
SANGIOVESE
SYRAH
ZINFANDEL

You'll also find some white varieties, mainly Chardonnay and Sauvignon Blanc. Devastated by the 2017 wildfires, the area looks to be rebuilding quickly.

—

PRICE TO RATING CHART

THE GRAPH INDICATES VIVINO USERS'
AVERAGE RATINGS FOR WINES AT
DIFFERENT PRICE POINTS IN
THIS AVA.

DATA POWERED BY VIVINO

ATLAS PEAK

PRICE TO RATING CHART

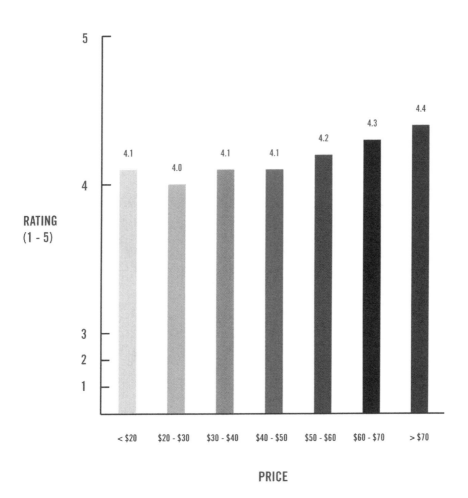

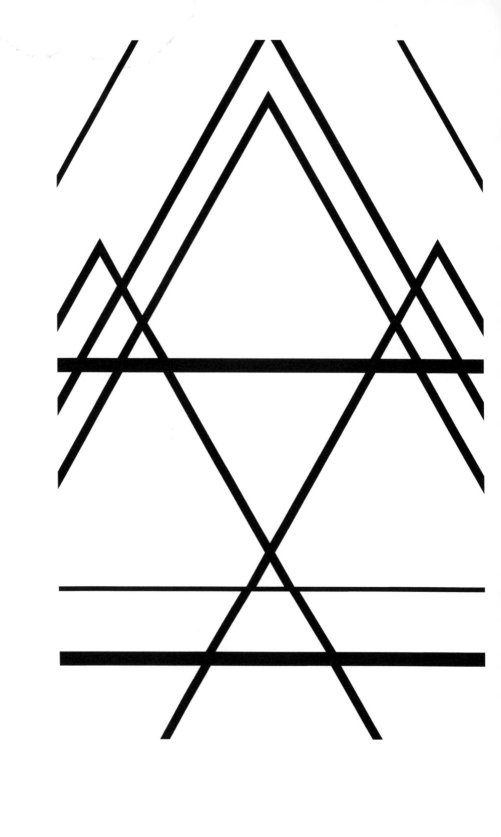

SOUTH TO NORTH

AVA 9:

OAKVILLE

▼

OAKVILLE
WINERIES & VINEYARDS

Acre
B Cellars
BOND
Cardinale
Cardinale Estate
Continuum
Dalla Valle Vineyards
Detert
Dolce
Far Niente
Futo Estate
Galerie
Gamble Family Vineyards
Gargiulo Vineyards
Ghost Block
Groth Vineyards & Winery
Harbison Estate Wines
Harlan Estate
Miner Family Winery
Napa Cellars
Nemerever Vineyards
Nickel & Nickel
Oakville Cross Wine
Oakville Ranch Vineyards
Oakville Winery
Opus One

Paradigm Winery
Plaza Del Dotto Winery
Plumpjack Winery
Promontory
Robert Mondavi Winery
Rudd
Saddleback Cellars
Screaming Eagle Winery
Silver Oak Cellars
Spoto Family Wines
Stanton Vineyards
Teaderman Vineyards
Tench Winery
The Mascot
Turnbull Cellars
Tusk Estates
Ulysses Vineyard
VHR
Villa Ragazzi
Vine Cliff Winery

The wine industry is dynamic. For up-to-date listings, please visit individual AVA websites.

Q&A

OAKVILLE

FAR NIENTE WINERY

NICOLE MARCHESI

WINEMAKER

WHAT DO YOU LIKE MOST ABOUT YOUR OAKVILLE?

I like the complexity of Oakville. For being a small sub-AVA there's actually quite a bit of diversity form east to west, from vineyard to vineyard, sometimes even from block to block. There are distinct profiles as well; on the west side, Far Niente's vineyard is planted on an alluvial fan that descends from the Mayacamas. The eastern side of Oakville has more volcanic influence. So there's a lot of variation, and it's pretty awesome to be working with such complexity, especially with Cabernet Sauvignon.

WHAT EFFECT DOES THE REGION HAVE ON THE GRAPES THAT ARE GROWN THERE?

One of the great things about Oakville is that it's in the middle of the valley, a transitional area where you're moving from the cooler southern part to the warmer northern part, so you get a little bit of the best of both worlds. There are nice cool nights and morning fog formed by the bay influence. That fog burns off mid-morning and we get some beautiful warm temperatures by the afternoon. Wine grapes need this warmth to ripen during the day, and the cool nights help to maintain color and acidy.

▼

WHAT CHARACTERISTICS WILL WE NOTICE WHEN TASTING A WINE FROM OAKVILLE AVA?

I'd say most winemakers are growing Cabernet Sauvignon. Because it is a later ripening varietal, you need some warmth to get it appropriately ripe and not have vegetal characteristics. Because of the cooler nights, we retain good acidity and tannin structure. It's a hallmark of Oakville. You can get substantial tannin but it's very high quality. They're big, rich wines that you can drink young, but there is tons of aging potential in Oakville Cabernets. My colleagues from other wineries and I all agree that they can be beautiful right out of the gate, with mixed berry, boysenberry and blackberry flavors, but all of them have tannin that makes them great for putting down. Its ageability is tremendous.

WHAT MIGHT PEOPLE MISUNDERSTAND ABOUT YOUR AVA?

In general, with Cabernet in Napa I think there is an assumption that everyone is making over-the-top, super-fruity wines. But I think that is a broad generalization about Napa Cabernet. I know from my experience in Oakville that there is a dedication to making nuanced, layered wines with appropriate fruit and tannin profiles.

WHAT ELSE DO YOU WANT PEOPLE TO KNOW ABOUT YOUR AVA?

I think in our AVA, we have always been pursuing balanced wines. If you taste wines from the last 10 years from many of the wineries in Oakville, there is definitely a focus on balance and appropriate tannic expression and fruit. Some producers want very fruit-driven wines, which you can have in Oakville. Others have a great balance of mixed berry fruit with other elements. Cabernet can have a slightly herbal edge to it, which some people really like. You'll often green tea and herbal notes.

One other thing that I really love about Oakville is that from the people side it's a pretty close-knit group of growers and wineries that try to come together and share and collaborate. People believe in the place, and they believe not only in making their own wineries better but sharing and collaborating and improving the AVA generally. It's a really nice community.

OAKVILLE

DRIVE THROUGH NAPA

CLIMATE

Moderately warm, with temperatures commonly in the mid-90s during high summer, but still strongly affected by night and early morning fog, which helps keep acidity levels high. The east side of the AVA receives warmer afternoon sun.

ELEVATION

130 to 1,000 feet.

RAINFALL

35 inches annually.

SOILS

Primarily sedimentary gravelly alluvial loams on the western side, with more volcanic but heavier soils on the eastern side. Low to moderate fertility and fairly deep, with average water retention.

PRINCIPAL VARIETIES & CHARACTERISTICS

Cabernet Sauvignon, Cabernet Franc, and Merlot: Ripe currant and mint flavors, rich texture and full, firm structure. Sauvignon Blanc: Full, steely, yet very fleshy.

▼

Oakville was the focus of California's first great wine boom, which happened almost a century before Robert Mondavi transformed Napa in the middle of the 20th century. When America's serious financial slump eased in the late 1870s, vineyards began to appear around this tiny central Napa community. Between 1878 and 1889, the village along the tracks was the hub of California's most important wine district.

Ohio-born Henry Walker Crabb helped transform Oakville into a premium wine district. Arriving in California at 25 in 1853, Crabb settled in San Lorenzo before moving to Napa in 1865. He purchased a 240-acre parcel in Oakville in 1868. By 1877, Crabb's 130-acre vineyard was producing 50,000 gallons of wine annually. He named his lucky vineyard To-Kalon, Greek for "most beautiful."

Others who benefitted from wine's first growth spurt included John Benson. In 1873, he bought 400 acres of Oakville land and planted an 84-acre vineyard. Three years later, in honor of his 15,000-gallon premiere vintage, he named his estate Far Niente, Italian for "without a care."

Most are more familiar with Oakville's more recent history-making chapter, which began in 1966, the year Robert Mondavi entered the picture in a big way. He had recently split from his family at another Napa Valley winery, selecting a spot on the To-Kalon property as the site for a spectacular new winery that would bear his name. It was the first significant new winery to open in Napa Valley since the end of Prohibition, and the beginning of the era when California wine would increasingly dominate world markets.

The climate of Oakville is unusual, the result of several weather influences. Cool ocean air mingles with warmer, drier inland air from the central San Joaquin Valley, creating a temperate Mediterranean climate in Oakville and giving it daily weather patterns that are ideal for growing quality grapes. Oakville also receives the full benefit of the afternoon Napa Valley sun. But when the thermometer begins to rise, marine breezes kick in and bring temperatures down quickly. Oakville is customarily about one degree cooler than Rutherford, three degrees cooler than St. Helena, and eight degrees cooler than Calistoga.

Three kinds of soil dominate the Oakville district. In the hills, bedrock is breaking down into mineral-rich residual soils. Just below the hills, alluvial soils are washed down from the adjoining hills. In the central valley near the river, fine loam has been carried down from upstream and deposited fairly evenly.

A list of Oakville's most prominent wineries is a veritable Napa pantheon:

ROBERT MONDAVI
JOSEPH HEITZ
GROTH
FAR NIENTE
OPUS ONE
DALLA VALLE
HARLAN ESTATE
SCREAMING EAGLE

▼

—

PRICE TO RATING CHART

THE GRAPH INDICATES VIVINO USERS'
AVERAGE RATINGS FOR WINES AT
DIFFERENT PRICE POINTS IN
THIS AVA.

DATA POWERED BY VIVINO

OAKVILLE

PRICE TO RATING CHART

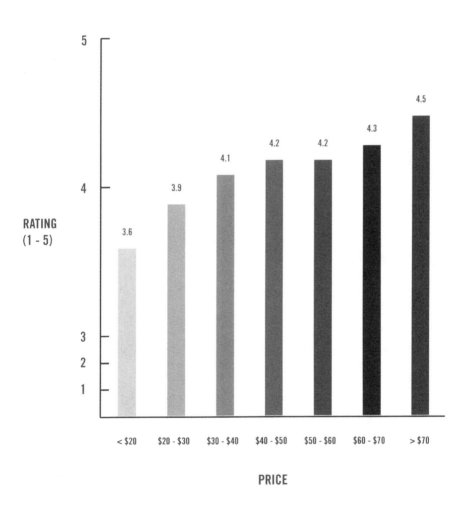

RATING (1 - 5)

Price	Rating
< $20	3.6
$20 - $30	3.9
$30 - $40	4.1
$40 - $50	4.2
$50 - $60	4.2
$60 - $70	4.3
> $70	4.5

PRICE

SOUTH TO NORTH

AVA 10:

RUTHERFORD

RUTHERFORD
WINERIES & VINEYARDS

Alpha Omega
Arbe Garbe Wines
Bacio Divino Cellars
Beaulieu Vineyard (BV)
Belle Glos
Bello Family Vineyards
Cakebread Cellars
Calder Wine Company
Caymus Vineyards
Conn Creek Winery
Conundrum Wines
Courtesan - Brigitte
Cultivar Wine
Dana Estates
Del Dotto Estate Winery
Elizabeth Spencer Winery
Emmolo Wines
Fleury Estate Winery
Foley Johnson Wines
Frog's Leap Winery
Gallegos Wines
Grand Wines Napa
Green & Red Vineyard
Grgich Hills Estate
HALL Wines
Hewitt Vineyard
Honig Vineyard and Winery
Hundred Acre
Inglenook
Jack Quinn Wines
Kuleto Estate Winery
Martin Estate
Mathew Bruno Wines

Metaphora Wines
Mumm Napa
Peju Province Winery
Pestoni Family Estate Winery
Quintessa Winery
Riverain Vineyards
Round Pond Estate
Rutherford Hill Winery
Rutherford Ranch Winery
S.R. Tonella Cellars
Scarecrow Wine
Sequoia Grove
Sloan Estate
St. Supery
Staglin Family Vineyard
Sullivan Vineyards
Tayson Pierce Wines
The Terraces
Tres Sabores
Trujillo Wines
Whitehall Lane Winery
Wicker Vineyards
William Harrison Wines
ZD Wines

The wine industry is dynamic. For up-to-date listings, please visit individual AVA websites.

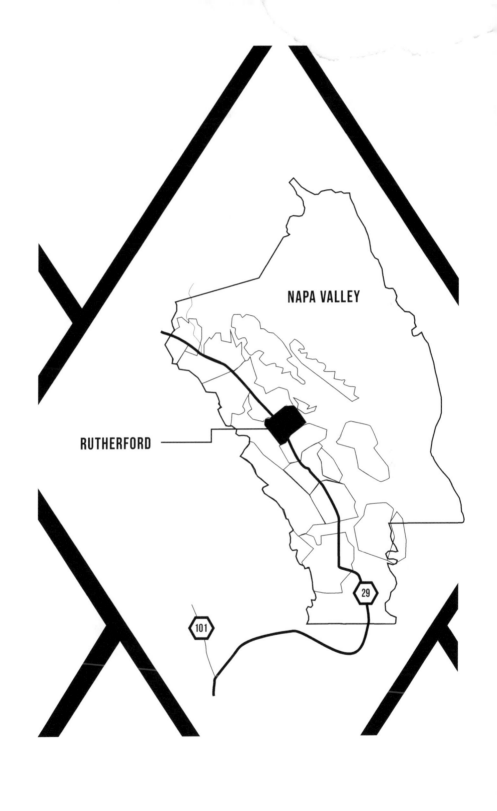

RUTHERFORD

GRGICH HILLS ESTATE

IVO JERAMAZ

WINEMAKER

WHAT DO YOU LIKE MOST ABOUT RUTHERFORD?

We have five estates in Napa from Carneros to Calistoga, totaling 365 acres, and I know each area well. We have 16 acres in Rutherford. The soil and climate here are very different from Yountville, which is only six miles south. It's much lighter, loamier there. Our soil is more clay, a bit more humid than Yountville, and it's next to the Vaca Mountains, so there's soil with lots of pebbles where we are, about halfway from Napa River to the mountains. Also, there is Bear Creek. It doesn't flow in the summer, but there is underground water there. It is an interesting area for us. We can easily dry farm. Bud break is often delayed, and so is everything else. This year we harvested in the middle of November.

WHAT EFFECT DOES YOUR REGION HAVE ON THE GRAPES THAT GROW HERE?

Rutherford wine is always more supple and approachable when it's young than wine from other places in this part of the valley. Yountville has more firm structure. Rutherford is more seductive. Right now for the '14 or '15 vintage, I would take Rutherford because it's ready to go. There's a forwardness in Rutherford that is not present in Yountville.

▼

WHAT WILL WE NOTICE WHEN TASTING A WINE FROM RUTHERFORD?

The wines here are not as structured as Yountville wines; they're a bit softer, with considerably higher pH. Many people love that style of wine. And the famous Rutherford dust – I find it hard to describe it, but you know it when you taste it. It's very personal for everybody. This is a good place for winemakers like me who prefer to stay away from extremes. I don't do plush wines that are high in alcohol and sugar. I don't do shock and awe wines. I like the more balanced style, and I find I can achieve it very well in Rutherford.

WHAT DO PEOPLE MISUNDERSTAND ABOUT YOUR AVA?

That there are lots of variables, not only here but in any AVA, that might have a greater effect on the taste of the wine than location on its own. Three winemakers might harvest the same vineyard at different times. Even though it is the same terroir, same vineyard, you cannot discount the influence of the harvest date or the winemaker. Also, in Napa, we don't have the advantage of hundreds of years of growing grapes in the same place, like they do in France. We have learned a lot in a very short time, but it will take a lot longer to know all the secrets of a particular vineyard's location.

WHAT ELSE DO YOU WANT PEOPLE TO KNOW ABOUT YOUR AVA?

If I could make one final point, although it must be obvious by now that I would say this: predicting the taste of an AVA is hard. Many people don't understand that what winemakers do is mainly farming. There is great unpredictability to many of the things that happen in the field and the winery from year to year. That is what makes wine fascinating, and makes it hard for me to talk precisely about style and those kinds of things. There are many, many variables, and that's what makes winemaking so fascinating.

RUTHERFORD

DRIVE THROUGH NAPA

CLIMATE

Moderately warm, influenced slightly by early morning fog. Western bench area is cooler, with less late afternoon sun, and regularly cooled by afternoon marine winds. Warmer than Oakville and Stags Leap District: summer peak temperatures are mid-90s, with a large diurnal swing.

ELEVATION

155 to 500 feet.

RAINFALL

38 inches annually.

SOILS

Western benchland is sedimentary, gravelly-sandy and alluvial, with good water retention and moderate fertility. The eastern side has more volcanic soils, moderately deep and more fertile.

PRINCIPAL VARIETIES & CHARACTERISTICS

Cabernet Sauvignon, Merlot, Cabernet Franc, Zinfandel: Intense cherry and mineral quality, with earthy, dusty qualities (sometimes referred to as "Rutherford dust"). Full, ripe flavors with strong hint of currant. Firm but not overwhelming tannins, good markers for extended aging.

▼

With the town of Rutherford as its bull's-eye, this mid-valley region is known for its unusual terroir, which especially affects the taste profile of Cabernet Sauvignon.

The well-drained soil is a mix of gravel, loam and sand with smaller amounts of volcanic deposits and marine sediments. The appellation is fairly small (about 6,650 acres in the center of Napa Valley), but it's a hotbed of iconic labels.

Rutherford undoubtedly belongs in the top tier of Napa Valley AVAs. It is located south of St. Helena and immediately north of Oakville, at the heart of the valley floor's wine-growing area. The town is named after Thomas Lewis Rutherford, who married Elizabeth Yount, granddaughter of Napa wine pioneer George C. Yount.

New York Times wine columnist Frank Prial makes a case for why Rutherford might be Napa's most illustrious AVA by listing who's there. "Among the wineries to be found in that rather small tract of real estate are Beaulieu, Inglenook, Niebaum-Coppola, Grgich Hills, Far Niente and Vichon; vineyard properties include the renowned Martha's Vineyard and Bella Oaks Vineyard, whose grapes are used by Heitz Cellars, the Bosche Vineyard, which supplies Freemark Abbey, and parcels owned by the Robert Mondavi, Pine Ridge and Joseph Phelps wineries."

Cabernet Sauvignon is the most widely planted grape here, and it's highly prized. The long, warm summer days encourage the loamy flavors that have made Napa's Cabernet Sauvignon famous, complemented by deeply supported, sumptuous fruit. Tannins are big but not harsh, one of the key characteristics that make Rutherford's Cabernets some of America's most highly acclaimed red wines.

▼

Then there's the prized "Rutherford Dust" taste. Here's how Winemaker Mike Smith defines it: "In Rutherford, the deeper soils and microclimates create longer growing seasons and 'hang time' that seem to round out the tannins in a soft, dusty style. This gives wines from the area a powdery 'fine dusty tannin' effect with hints of plump cocoa powder. It is an absolutely addictive element in these wines."

There's an ongoing dispute about the origin of the term. Some think that Andre Tchelistcheff came up with it when he worked at Beaulieu Vineyards. Others say Maynard Amerine used it first while a faculty member in Viticulture and Enology at UC Davis.

Cabernet's Bordeaux brethren, Merlot, Malbec, Cabernet Franc and Petit Verdot, are also grown here, and though they're usually blended you can find them in single-varietal form, too.

Rutherford's boundaries stretch from the base of the Mayacamas Mountains to the Silverado Trail at the bottom of the Vaca Mountains.

Rutherford's afternoons in summer are sometimes cooled by maritime fog flowing northwards up the valley. This moderating factor gives Rutherford's grapes, especially Cabernet Sauvignon, a sought-after balance of flavor and acidity. Soils of sandy loam, deep and well drained, are found throughout the AVA, although clay dominates closer to the banks of the Napa River and Conn Creek. Another characteristic of the terroir: hints of eucalyptus and mint.

Chardonnay and Sauvignon Blanc are grown in the Rutherford AVA, but they're almost an afterthought. Cabernet is king.

▼

—

PRICE TO RATING CHART

THE GRAPH INDICATES VIVINO USERS'
AVERAGE RATINGS FOR WINES AT
DIFFERENT PRICE POINTS IN
THIS AVA.

DATA POWERED BY VIVINO

RUTHERFORD

PRICE TO RATING CHART

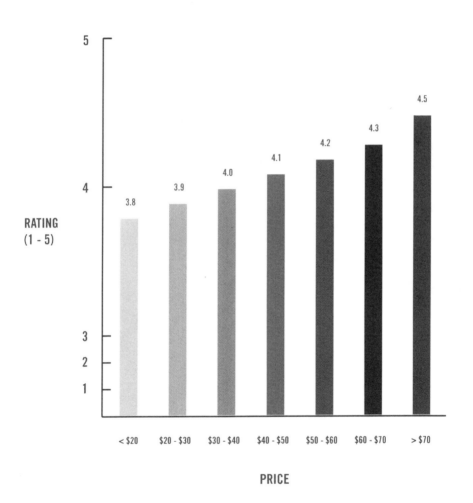

RATING
(1 - 5)

PRICE

< $20 — 3.8
$20 - $30 — 3.9
$30 - $40 — 4.0
$40 - $50 — 4.1
$50 - $60 — 4.2
$60 - $70 — 4.3
> $70 — 4.5

SOUTH TO NORTH

AVA 11:

CHILES VALLEY

▼

CHILES VALLEY
WINERIES & VINEYARDS

Brown Estate
Maxville
Nichelini
Rustridge Vineyard & Winery
Volker Eisele Family Estate

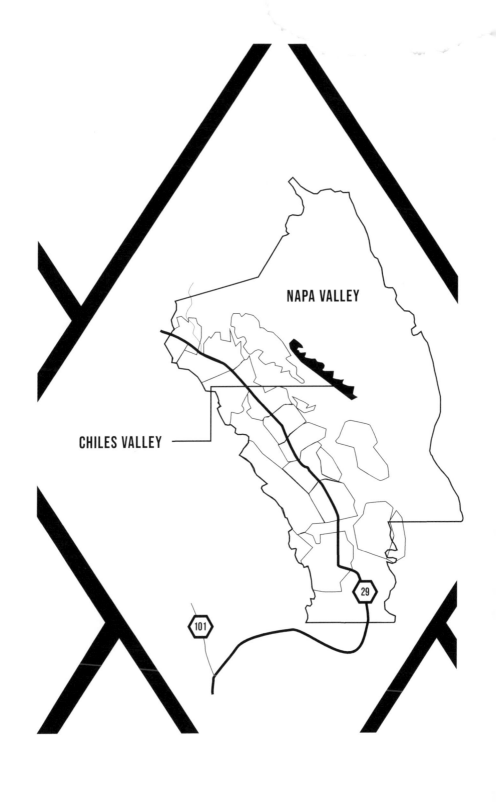

AVA 11

CHILES VALLEY

DRIVE THROUGH NAPA

CLIMATE

Warm summer days (mid-80s) but due to higher elevation and nocturnal fog in the summer, quite chilly at night (below 50). With cold winters and cool springs, as well as strong winds, harvest comes later than on the valley floor.

ELEVATION

600 to 1,200 feet.

RAINFALL

35 inches annually.

SOILS

On the valley floor, primarily alluvial soils with silty-clay composition of marine origin, and good fertility. Hillsides show more clay-loam and stony-clay composition, mostly marine in origin, with some volcanic outcropping, and less fertility.

PRINCIPAL VARIETIES & CHARACTERISTICS

Cabernet Sauvignon, Merlot, Cabernet Franc, Zinfandel. Cabernets are lush yet not overly fruity, with good acidity, firm tannins, and distinctive cherry-blackberry flavors. Merlot typically has vibrant black cherry flavors mixed with a touch of cocoa.

▼

In 1841, Joseph Ballinger Chiles received a land grant from the Mexican government for this tiny and narrow valley, barely eight miles long and three-quarters of a mile wide. It took four decades, though, before Swiss immigrants finally planted vineyards in the area, which was known mainly as a source of tin and gypsum during the first half of the 19th century.

The Nichelini family established one of the first wineries in 1890. Louis Martini planted a vineyard here in the 1930s, although his winery remained on Highway 29 south of St. Helena. In the 1970s, Jay Heminway and Volker Eisele brought the modern era of viticulture to the area. They helped establish nested appellation status for the valley in 1999.

The Vaca Mountain Range surrounds Chiles Valley, Napa's easternmost wine region, and its vineyards lie mostly between 600 and 1,200 feet above sea level, although a few hillside vineyards lie at 1,700 feet or more. Lower elevations (up to 1,000 feet) tend to get enveloped in fog frequently. Nights can be quite cold – the west-lying hills aren't high, inviting the Pacific marine influence to flow in unimpeded.

Only 750 acres of its 4,000-acre area are planted to wine grapes. E&J Gallo owns about 330 acres, including the well-regarded Martini Ghost Pines Ranch.

Because of its relative remoteness, Chiles Valley is one of the least visited Napa Valley regions. Wine tourism isn't huge here, although it is growing. The drive up to the valley, though, is fascinating. You'll pass some of the cult wineries on Pritchard Hill.

Chiles Valley is cooler than most other wine regions in Napa. Zinfandel and Sauvignon Blanc thrive. So does Cabernet Sauvignon; Brown Estate and Eisele are producing fine examples of the variety here.

ZINFANDELS FROM CHILES VALLEY HAVE A SPICY AND FRUIT-FORWARD CHARACTER, BUT THEY'RE NOT UNBALANCED OR OVER THE TOP. CABERNETS FROM THIS AREA, TOO, PICK UP THAT UNIQUE SPICINESS.

Volker Eisele's Cabernets are often a good example of this flavor profile. Chardonnays from Chiles Valley have recently been getting more attention.

SOUTH TO NORTH

AVA 12:

ST. HELENA

ST. HELENA
WINERIES & VINEYARDS

Ad Vivum
Allora Vineyards
Accendo Cellars
Adler Deutsch Vineyard
Alpha Omega Winery
Anderson Conn Valley Vineyards
Anomaly Vineyards
Arns
AuburnJames Winery
Ballentine Vineyards
Barbour Vineyards
Benessere
Beringer
Bevan Cellars
Boeschen Vineyards
Boich Family Cellar
Buehler Vineyards
Calafia Wines
Casa Nuestra Winery
Chappellet
Charles Krug
Chase Family Cellars
Chateau Boswell
Clif Family
Conn Creek Winery
Corison Winery
Crocker & Starr Wines
Dakota Shy
Delectus
Duckhorn
Edge Hill
Ehlers Estate
Faust
Flora Springs
Flying Horse Winery
Freemark Abbey Winery
HALL Wines
Heitz Cellar
Howell Mountain Vineyards
Hunnicut
Joseph Phelps

Kelham
Louis M. Martini
Markham Vineyards
Merryvale Vineyards
Merus
Monticello Vineyards
Morlet Family Vineyards
Orin Swift
Palladian
Parallel
Pellet Estate
Prager Winery and Port Works
Raymond Vineyard & Cellar
Revana Family Vineyard
Reverie
Rombauer Vineyards
Saint Helena Winery
Salvestrin
Seavey
Sinegal Estate Winery
Spottswoode Estate
Taplin Cellars
The Prisoner Wine Company
Titus Vineyards
Trinchero Napa Valley
Trujillo Wines
V Madrone
V. Sattui Winery
VGS Chateau Potelle
Varozza Vineyards
Vineyard 29
William Cole Vineyards
Young Inglewood

The wine industry is dynamic. For up-to-date listings, please visit individual AVA websites.

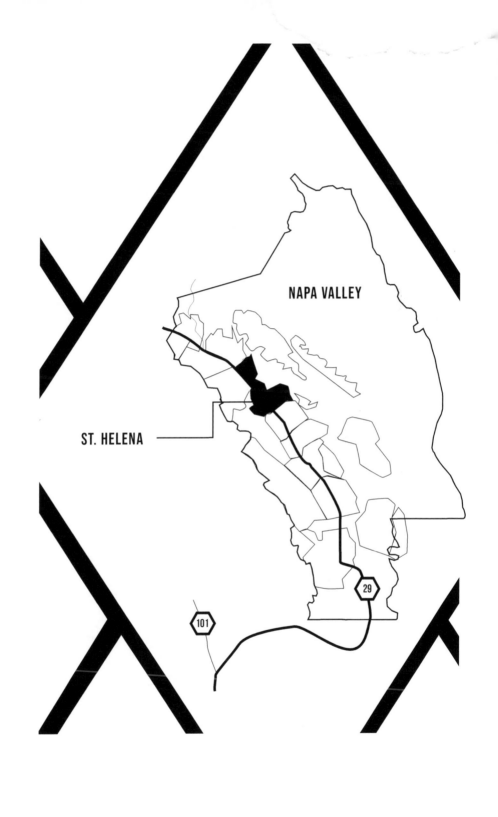

NAPA VALLEY

ST. HELENA

101

29

Q & A

ST. HELENA

RAYMOND VINEYARDS

JEAN–CHARLES BOISSET

OWNER

AS A WINEMAKER WHAT DO YOU LIKE MOST ABOUT ST. HELENA?

What I love about it is the neighborhood. This is the heart of Napa, with Rutherford at the epicenter. I love Oakville, too. So St. Helena's geographic location in middle of the valley is the perfect place. The grapes we can grow here have elegance and finesse; they're very seductive and refined, ethereal and intellectual. I also love the blend of hillside and floor. We have the best of both worlds.

WHAT EFFECT DOES YOUR REGION HAVE ON THE GRAPES THAT GROW HERE?

I think we're very fortunate here. From a climate standpoint, there's some heat during the day balanced by cool nights, so we get great ripeness and bright acidity to make elegant, age-worthy wines. And the soil is not too heavy. It makes our wine more ethereal.

WHAT WILL WE NOTICE WHEN TASTING A WINE FROM YOUR AVA?

I find the wine to be very inviting, and the finish leaves you with an indelible impression. I've tried a lot of St. Helena wines against Bordeaux, and it compares favorably. St. Helena wines are sophisticated and elegant, refined and silky in texture. Tannins are very well integrated. They're much more a part of the full-out flavor profile instead of being too invasive. A St. Helena wine is always a pleaser. Not too personality-driven, but definitely all Napa.

WHAT DO PEOPLE MISUNDERSTAND ABOUT YOUR AVA?

People tend to go back to Rutherford and Oakville and Calistoga because those wines are bigger. I think what we need to communicate is finesse and savoir-faire. More East Coast people love St. Helena. Also Asians and Europeans. We also need to explain that there's a large commitment to biodynamic agriculture here. I think we need to explain the need for food wines rather than big wines.

▼

WHAT ELSE DO YOU WANT PEOPLE TO KNOW ABOUT YOUR AVA?

That our wines aren't in your face or huge. I think it's important not to be obsessed with the percentage of alcohol on the label. Wines need to be food friendly; they can't just be a fruit bomb and an alcoholic bomb. The idea of life is harmony: the dialogue and conversation between the solids and the liquids, the food and the wine. Being true to the terroir is crucial. Winemakers need to be careful that it's not just all about themselves and their story. We need to have a sense of abnegation, of being more humble and letting the terroir do its best to express itself. Also, organic and biodynamic farming, especially in our industry, will become vitally important in the coming years. Many St. Helena grape growers and winemakers are at the forefront of this movement.

ST. HELENA

DRIVE THROUGH NAPA

CLIMATE

Warm, due to greater protection from western hills, with little fog or wind. This is the narrowest part of the Napa Valley floor, so there's more heat reflection from the hillsides. Mid-summer temperature peak is often in the mid-to-high 90s.

ELEVATION

200 to 475 feet.

RAINFALL

38 to 40 inches annually.

SOILS

South and west borders are more sedimentary gravel-clay soils, with lower fertility and moderate water retention. Further north and to the east the soils are prevalently volcanic in origin. They're also deeper and more fertile.

PRINCIPAL VARIETIES & CHARACTERISTICS

Cabernet Sauvignon, Cabernet Franc, Merlot: deep, ripe, often jammy flavors, with firm tannins for structure and acid for long cellaring. Appealing aromas of currant and black fruit. Syrah: Fleshy, supple and slightly earthy. Zinfandel: Blackberry-like, well-structured. Sauvignon Blanc: fresh and forward, with hints of passion fruit and lemon; crisp and fresh; not grassy.

▼

St. Helena, named after the nearby 4,345-foot-tall mountain, is one of the Napa Valley's seminal appellations. Designated in 1995, it is known for its superior Cabernet Sauvignon and Merlot, and it's home to some iconic names, including Beringer, Joseph Phelps, Turley and Duckhorn Vineyards.

Grape growing started very early in St. Helena, dating back to the Spanish colonial period. In 1841, British immigrant Edward Bale, the former Surgeon-In-Chief of the Mexican Army under General Mariano Vallejo, was granted the Rancho Carne Humana, which occupied the land between what is now Rutherford and Calistoga. Bale and his new bride, Vallejo's niece, promptly planted Mission grapes and watched them thrive. Today, part of that land is known as Beckstoffer Las Piedras vineyard, and it's one of the most acclaimed in Napa Valley.

The town and AVA start where Napa Valley begins to narrow about 15 miles north of the town of Napa. At this point, the mountains of the Vaca and Mayacamas ranges begin to pinch into the valley, with Spring Mountain and Diamond Mountain in the west not far from Howell Mountain in the east. Rutherford and Oakville, two of Napa's most prestigious appellations, lie just to the south.

The St. Helena AVA boundaries are defined by Zinfandel Lane to the south, Bale Lane to the north, the intersection of Howell Mountain and Conn Valley Road to the east and the 400-foot elevation line of the Mayacamas Mountain range to the west.

THIS 9,000-ACRE AVA IS HOME TO MORE THAN 30 WINERIES, INCLUDING SOME THAT FIGURE PROMINENTLY IN THE HISTORY OF NAPA.

First among these is Beringer, one of California's oldest continuously operating wineries, founded by Jacob Beringer and his brother Frederick in 1875. Not far from Beringer is the Charles Krug winery, established by a talented German-American winemaker who is sometimes called "the father of Napa wine."

St. Helena feels little of the marine effect of southern Napa; it is one of Napa's warmer appellations, surpassed only by Calistoga, which lies even farther up the valley. It has proven to be an ideal spot for Bordeaux varieties, and it's long been an excellent place for Zinfandel as well. White wines are not common in St. Helena, but Sauvignon Blanc is making some inroads.

▼

—

PRICE TO RATING CHART

THE GRAPH INDICATES VIVINO USERS'
AVERAGE RATINGS FOR WINES AT
DIFFERENT PRICE POINTS IN
THIS AVA.

DATA POWERED BY VIVINO

ST. HELENA

PRICE TO RATING CHART

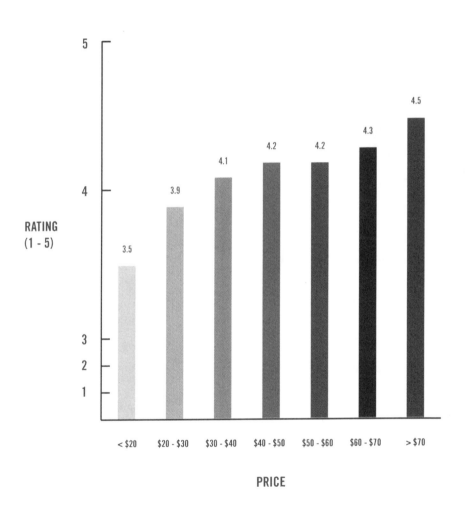

RATING (1 - 5)

Price	Rating
< $20	3.5
$20 - $30	3.9
$30 - $40	4.1
$40 - $50	4.2
$50 - $60	4.2
$60 - $70	4.3
> $70	4.5

PRICE

SOUTH TO NORTH

AVA 13:

SPRING MOUNTAIN

▼

SPRING MOUNTAIN
WINERIES & VINEYARDS

Barnett
Behrens
Cain
Castellucci
Fantesca
Juslyn
Keenan Winery
Lokoya
Marston
Newton Vineyard
Paloma
Peacock Vineyards
Pride Mountain
Ritchie Creek
Robert Keenan
Schoolhouse
Schweiger
Sherwin
Smith-Madrone
Spring Mountain Vineyard
Stony Hill
Terra Valentine
Vineyard 7&8

The wine industry is dynamic. For up-to-date listings, please visit individual AVA websites.

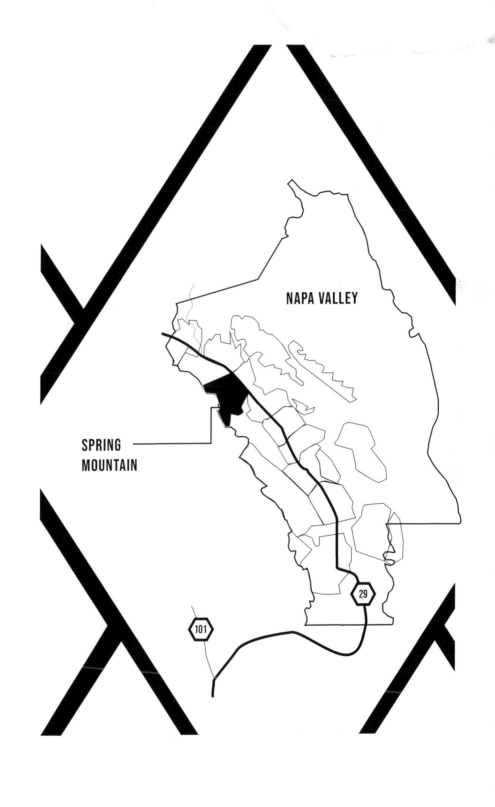

NAPA VALLEY

SPRING
MOUNTAIN

29

101

ABOUT

SPRING MOUNTAIN

SMITH-MADRONE VINEYARDS

STUART SMITH

CO-FOUNDER, VINEYARD MANAGER, WINEMAKER

AS A WINEMAKER WHAT DO YOU LIKE MOST ABOUT SPRING MOUNTAIN?

It all comes down to site, soil and climate. The soils here are mostly Aiken Stony Clay loam, which are volcanic-based, well drained and fairly deep for mountain soils. The geology here is what's called Franciscan Assemblage. That is a very, very old formation. When I first bought the property in 1971, we didn't know anything about any of that. But we knew the soil was very good, giving moderate fertility but not too much vigor. And the soils are stable. They don't slide.

The climate is interesting: In the summer, whatever it is in the valley floor, we're the opposite. We're cool when it's warm, warm when it's cool. During the growing season when the valley gets very hot, we are 7 or 8 degrees cooler. Early in the morning in August and September, we are mostly above the fog. So we get the sunlight that comes directly from the sun, then the sun that bounces off the fog.

A couple of times a year we also get an inversion on the mountain where it stays quite warm up here relative to the valley floor.

That can happen during the summer: June through August.

▼

WHAT EFFECT DOES YOUR REGION HAVE ON THE GRAPES THAT GROW HERE?

Not having those high temperatures on a regular basis is a good thing. With the soils, and not having a lot of water on the mountain, we don't get as big a crop as they do on the valley floor. With lower fertility and less water availability we tend to produce berries that are smaller. And a lot of flavor and color are in those smaller berries. There is a greater skin-to-juice ratio. That is common to most mountain vineyards.

WHAT WILL WE NOTICE WHEN TASTING A WINE FROM YOUR AVA?

There is something about mountain-grown fruit that I cannot adequately describe, something inherently different. It's in the way that my wines don't express oak in the same way valley floor grapes do when made into wine. I tend to think it's from the lack of fertility. The grapes are struggling to be expressive. Also, by not having enough water, the vines go from a vegetative to a ripening cycle on a more natural basis, a little earlier than valley floor fruit. I think the differences are more structural than flavor-based.

WHAT DO PEOPLE MISUNDERSTAND ABOUT YOUR AVA?

We'd like people to understand that even though we own expensive property, none of us are making a huge amount of money. When I used to teach winemaking back in the '80s I would say, "If you want to make money, don't go into the wine business." If you're really dedicated, you're going to have to give up a lot and work eight days a week during harvests. You may be sitting on a fair amount of wealth, but you don't get to spend it.

WHAT ELSE DO YOU WANT PEOPLE TO KNOW ABOUT YOUR AVA?

I'd say that one of the interesting things about Spring Mountain, Diamond Mountain, Mount Veeder and Howell Mountain is that we're mostly family-owned wineries. And I think that has significance. There is something about a family-owned winery — it makes wine that has more character and distinction. It has an ephemeral sense of art. Creativity really flows when the grower is also the owner and the winemaker.

SPRING MOUNTAIN

DRIVE THROUGH NAPA

CLIMATE

Cool to moderate depending on elevation and aspect. Most vineyards sit above the fog line, providing warmer nights and cooler days than the valley floor. Typical mid-summer high temperatures reach 85 degrees.

ELEVATION

600 to 2,600 feet.

RAINFALL

40 to 50 inches annually.

SOILS

Primarily sedimentary; weathered sandstone/ shale, loamy and friable in texture. Drainage is high, fertility low.

PRINCIPAL VARIETIES & CHARACTERISTICS

Cabernet Sauvignon, Cabernet Franc, Merlot, Zinfandel: Powerful, firm, blackberry-currant flavors and often richly tannic, with excellent acidity for aging. Chardonnay: Lean, firm and not as fruity as those of the valley floor, revealing more citrus and stone fruit flavors.

On Napa's western flank you'll find Spring Mountain District, nestled in a low spot in the Mayacamas Mountains. It was one of the first regions of Napa to support vineyards, as early as the Civil War years.

In 1874 German immigrant Charles Lemme planted the first significant commercial vineyard, a 25-acre tract south of York Creek. By the 1880s Spring Mountain supported several large and successful vineyards; Jacob and Frederick Beringer planted here, and an influential early winemaker, wealthy San Francisco banker Tiburcio Parrott, made award-winning wines from Spring Mountain fruit in the 1890s.

Spring Mountain's post-Prohibition resurgence began in 1946 when Fred and Eleanor McCrea established a small vineyard near Mill Creek. Seven years later they opened Stony Hill, a very successful winery. By the 1970s, several independent-minded and talented winemakers had established themselves in the area. Prominent wineries included Ritchie Creek, Yverdon, Spring Mountain Vineyard, Smith-Madrone and Robert Keenan.

The vineyards here produce mostly red wine grapes; Cabernet Sauvignon is the predominant variety. Although they're often big and fruit-forward, Spring Mountain District wines usually offer more soft-shouldered tannins than reds from the valley floor.

The AVA is one of the more northerly in Napa, and its 8,600 acres are varied: undulating hills, scrubland, even some forest just south of Diamond Mountain District and Calistoga. The St. Helena AVA (and township) can be found below, on the valley floor. Although it was awarded AVA status fairly early, in 1993, Spring Mountain District doesn't share quite the same prestige or recognition of nearby AVAs.

Elevation is key in Spring Mountain District.

Most vineyards have been planted between 1,300 and 2,000 feet above sea level, so they're above the usual fog line. But that's a double-edged sword: those upper reaches don't benefit from the fog's cooling effects either.

Weather is complex here. Summer afternoons can be downright cool, and you might see waterfalls of fog arcing over the western ridges and flowing down through the canyons. At night, cool air and fog settle on the floor of the valley, pushing warm air to higher elevations. Mornings warm more quickly on Spring Mountain than on the valley floor because it lies above the morning fog line. The result is warm daily high temperatures and moderately warm nighttime temperatures. These conditions allow sugar accumulation in the berry to keep pace with flavor development.

Spring Mountain receives 10 to 15 inches more annual rainfall than the Napa Valley floor or the eastern slopes of the valley. Total annual precipitation can reach 70 to 95 inches in the wettest years.

Overall, the climate produces an unusually long growing season. Bud break occurs in mid-March, veraison happens around July 1, and harvest takes place from mid-September to November.

Spring Mountain's topography is varied, and its vineyards can be found in many of its hillocks and valleys. The soil can be rocky and poor in nutrients, subjecting the vines to a great deal of stress and forcing their roots systems to go deep for sustenance. The result: low yields, small berries, and exquisitely concentrated flavors.

Spring Mountain sustains many varietals beyond the expected Cabernet Sauvignon. Cabernet Franc, Merlot, Zinfandel, Riesling and Chardonnay do well here. Smith-Madrone has enjoyed considerable success with its Riesling.

▼

—

PRICE TO RATING CHART

THE GRAPH INDICATES VIVINO USERS'
AVERAGE RATINGS FOR WINES AT
DIFFERENT PRICE POINTS IN
THIS AVA.

DATA POWERED BY VIVINO

SPRING MOUNTAIN

PRICE TO RATING CHART

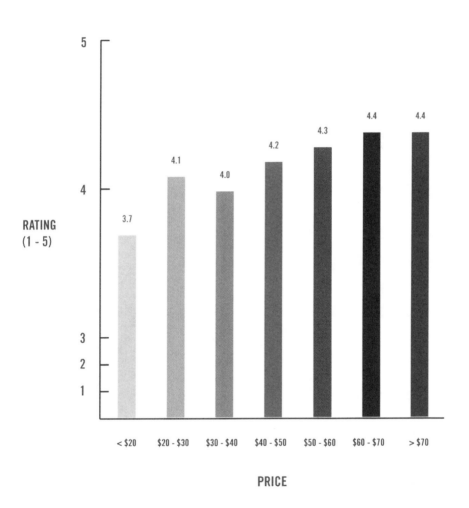

RATING
(1 - 5)

PRICE

SOUTH TO NORTH

AVA 14:

HOWELL MOUNTAIN

HOWELL MOUNTAIN
WINERIES & VINEYARDS

ADAMVS
Aloft Wine
Amizetta Winery
Angwin Estate Vineyards
Arkenstone
Black Sears Estate Wines
Blue Hall Vineyard
Bravante Vineyards
Bremer Family Winery
CADE Estate Winery
Charles Krug Winery
Cimarossa
Dunn Vineyards
Haber Family Vineyards
Hall Wines
Hindsight Wines
Howell at the Moon
Howell Mountain Vineyards
Jones Family
KIND Cellars
KrisTodd Vineyards
La Jota Vineyard Co.
Ladera Vineyards
Lamborn Family Vineyards
Mending Wall
Mirror Napa Valley
Moone-Tsai Wines
O'Shaughnessy Estate Winery
Outpost Estate Winery
Paravel Wines
Piña Napa Valley
Poetic Moon
Press Cellars
Prim Family Vineyard
Red Cap Vineyards
Red Thread Wines
Retro Cellars

Robert Craig Winery
Robert Foley Vineyards
Round Two Wines
Saunter Wines
Seek Wines
Selah Wines | Blanton Family Vineyards
SPENCE
Summit Lake Vineyards & Winery
TreeBottom Wines

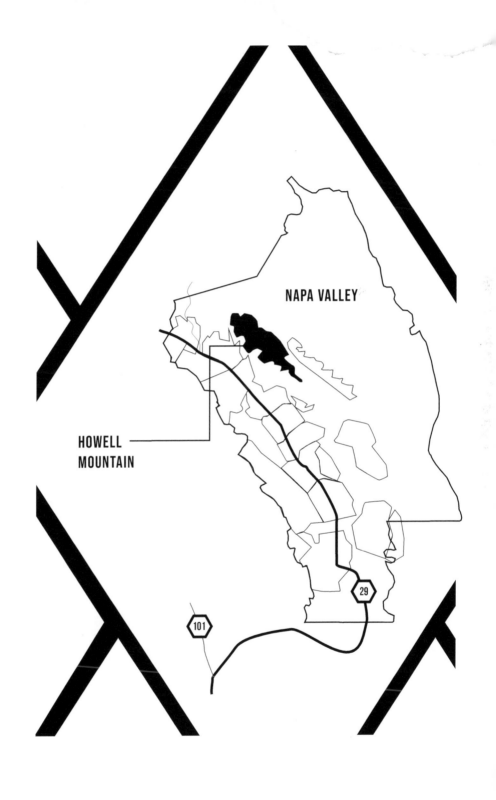

NAPA VALLEY

HOWELL
MOUNTAIN

101

29

HOWELL MOUNTAIN

CADE WINERY

DANIELLE CYROT

WINEMAKER

WHAT DO YOU LIKE MOST ABOUT HOWELL MOUNTAIN?

There are a couple of things that make it unique.
The first is elevation. We're high, about 1,450 feet.
The second important feature is the soils on Howell
Mountain, which are mostly volcanic and very old.
I think that definitely plays a part in what you taste in
the glass. And the microclimate of Howell Mountain –
we have this occurrence where the valley floor will be
covered in fog and you get to our elevation and all of a
sudden you're above the clouds and we're 10 degrees
warmer than the valley floor for three or four hours.
All of that makes Howell Mountain wines unique.

WHAT EFFECT DOES YOUR REGION HAVE ON THE GRAPES THAT GROW HERE?

Howell Mountain's many hillsides make it challenging
to farm. We can't do all of the operations that we need
to viticulturally with tractors. You have to do it by hand.
There are some blocks that are inaccessible by tractor
that are completely farmed by hand. One person has
to work on the vine and do multiple things to it
simultaneously, because we can't do that many
passes. It's physically impractical.

▼

Also, because these blocks are on hillsides, they're not evenly planted. It's not flat; there are trees. On the valley floor, harvest is easy. Here we don't pick the whole block at the same time. The top of the vineyard may be completely different from the middle and bottom. And there's forest surrounding the vineyard that varies conditions from row to row. Sometimes I'm picking blocks three to five times in order to insure that we're getting all the fruit at its peak.

WHAT WILL WE NOTICE WHEN TASTING A WINE FROM YOUR HOWELL MOUNTAIN?

I mostly work with Cabernet Sauvignon; I also do a little bit of Malbec. Cabernet from Howell Mountain has more of a red fruit character than in other districts. You'll get cherry and raspberry and even strawberry. Howell Mountain reds have great structure, firm tannins and wonderful intensity. I wouldn't say there's minerality, but there is a structure to Howell Mountain wines that you don't get in other wines. And that structure allows for ageing. I think that Howell wines could lay down in the bottle for 15 to 20 years and you will still have this great structure that pairs really well with steaks and meat.

We do make a Cabernet for which I select the best of the best — my favorite barrels and blocks. Those wines tend to have black cherry and boysenberry and blueberry characteristics, with a nice intensity and weight to the palate. I would describe it as a rounded structure.

If you're paying attention to the phenolics you can get a spectrum of fruit flavors on Howell Mountain, and an intense color as well.

WHAT DO PEOPLE MISUNDERSTAND ABOUT YOUR AVA?

Some people are shocked by our prices, but they don't understand what is going into each bottle. We don't make a $50 bottle of Howell Mountain Cabernet. We are above that price point. But I think what we're hopefully delivering on is quality in the bottle. I know everything that goes into making these wines: the viticulture, the care, the barrels we use. Everything we do is very traditional. We're not trying to cut corners on anything.

WHAT ELSE DO YOU WANT PEOPLE TO KNOW ABOUT YOUR AVA?

There are fewer than 20 wineries on Howell Mountain. But it is a unique appellation that has produced some pretty spectacular wines. They're special bottles for big occasions, and you can lay them down for many years.

HOWELL MOUNTAIN

DRIVE THROUGH NAPA

CLIMATE

Located above the fog line on the eastern side of the valley, Howell Mountain is warmer and drier than other AVAs, with more hours of sunshine and little marine influence.

ELEVATION

1,400 to 2,600 feet.

RAINFALL

40 to 50 inches annually.

SOILS

There are two main soil types on Howell Mountain: decomposed volcanic ash (called "tufa") and red clay. Average topsoil depth is 12 to 24 inches. Drainage is excellent, fertility is low.

PRINCIPAL VARIETIES & CHARACTERISTICS

Cabernet Sauvignon, Merlot, Zinfandel: Powerful, firm, blackberry-currant flavors and often richly tannic, with excellent acidity for aging. Chardonnay, Viognier: Sinewy, firm and not as fruity as those of the valley floor, revealing more citrus and stone fruit flavors.

▼

Farmer Isaac Howell arrived in northeastern Napa in 1847 and gave the area its name, but it wasn't until the 1880s that grapes were planted in this steep, rocky and challenging region. Frenchmen Jean Brun and Jean V. Chaix planted extensive vineyards and opened a winery, quickly establishing wines of enviable quality. (Ladera Vineyards now occupies the original winery.) Because they also owned an Oakville operation (today the location of The Napa Wine Co.), they were among the most successful local wine businesses during the boom of the 1880s.

Other iconic winegrowers established operations here: Charles Krug, W.A.C. Smith, Frederick Hess, and W.S. Keyes, who started Liparita Vineyards and later La Jota. By the end of the 1880s there were more than 600 acres of wine grapes planted, and the vineyards on Howell Mountain had developed an excellent reputation despite its famously difficult growing conditions.

Beginning in 1889, the Howell Mountain region became known to the wider world when Brun & Chaix won a Bronze medal at the Paris World Competition. In 1909, Keyes took gold and bronze, and Hess nabbed the bronze for his La Jota Vineyard Company Blanco table wine. At the St. Louis Exposition in 1904, Keyes repeated his Paris triumph, winning the grand prize for his red wine. More than a century ago, Howell Mountain was the first world-famous region within Napa.

Howell Mountain was the second designated appellation in Napa when it was named on Dec. 30, 1983, and many upper-end Napa wineries source fruit from here. In recent years, the number of wineries on Howell Mountain has steadily grown; now there are well over 50. Many have stunning views down the valley.

The vineyards of Howell Mountain, many on rocky and undulating land, can be found anywhere between 600 and 2,600 feet above sea level; most are in a sweet spot between 1,400 and 2,200 feet, just above the fog line. Many largely treeless hilltop locations permit long hours of sunshine, sometimes all day. Because of its altitude, evening temperatures on Howell Mountain are generally warmer and daytime temperatures are cooler than the valley floor. This levels out thermal spikes that tend to be more exaggerated at lower elevations. The result is a gradual growth process that produces small, concentrated grapes and ultimately more robust, complex but well-balanced wines.

HOWELL MOUNTAIN WINES HAVE FIRM STRUCTURE AND BACKBONE, VARIETAL INTENSITY, AND THEY AGE EXTREMELY WELL.

The taste profile of Howell Mountain red wines is famously vigorous, with aromas of ripe mountain berries, dark currants, and floral notes, expressing themselves in a dusty, earthy minerality. The fruit components are very dark in flavor and color with a lot of black cherry, blackberry, plum, chocolate and mocha. Howell Mountain wines also contain hints of spice, tobacco and mineral.

▼

—

PRICE TO RATING CHART

THE GRAPH INDICATES VIVINO USERS'
AVERAGE RATINGS FOR WINES AT
DIFFERENT PRICE POINTS IN
THIS AVA.

DATA POWERED BY VIVINO

HOWELL MOUNTAIN

PRICE TO RATING CHART

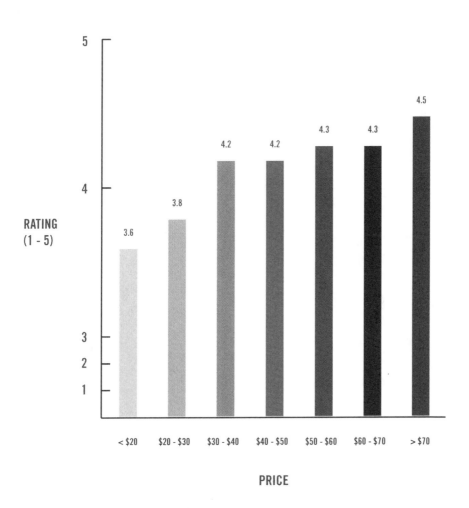

RATING
(1 - 5)

| < $20 | $20 - $30 | $30 - $40 | $40 - $50 | $50 - $60 | $60 - $70 | > $70 |
| 3.6 | 3.8 | 4.2 | 4.2 | 4.3 | 4.3 | 4.5 |

PRICE

SOUTH TO NORTH

AVA 15:

DIAMOND MOUNTAIN

DIAMOND MOUNTAIN

WINERIES & VINEYARDS

Andrew Geoffrey Vineyards
Checkerboard Vineyards
Diamond Creek Vineyards
Dyer Vineyard
Joseph Cellars Winery
Mueller Family Vineyards
Reverie
Schramsberg Vineyards
Seaver Vineyards
The Vineyardist
Vineyard 511
von Strasser Winery
Wallis Family Estate

The wine industry is dynamic. For up-to-date listings, please visit individual AVA websites.

DIAMOND
MOUNTAIN

NAPA VALLEY

101

29

ABOU-

DIAMOND MOUNTAIN

DYER VINEYARD

DAWNINE & BILL DYER

OWNERS, GRAPE GROWERS AND WINEMAKERS

WHAT DO YOU LIKE MOST ABOUT DIAMOND MOUNTAIN?

On Diamond Mountain we get the intensity and power of mountain vineyards with a deep core of structure and balance – it's a natural site. Our vineyard is between 600 and 900 feet (above sea level). We can get fog, but it's not the primary characteristic of the region.

An interesting thing about Diamond Mountain is that while people think Napa Valley runs north to south, it's not 100 percent true. It runs north-south until St. Helena then it veers to the west. By the time you get to our area, you're as close to the ocean as you are to the bay. There are some gaps that come over from Santa Rosa and Petaluma where we get the ocean influence. That dogleg to the west makes all the difference. We get as much cooling influence from the west as we do from the south. The diurnal swing here can be pronounced, from the 90s in the day to the 50s at night.

WHAT EFFECT DOES DIAMOND MOUNTAIN HAVE ON THE GRAPES THAT GROW HERE?

Our soils are uniquely volcanic with deep drainage, and our location in the slightly cooler western hills provides an opportunity for the grapes to develop flavors over a long growing season. Diamond Mountain wines have the classic structure of wines grown in volcanic soils. We have reasonable water-holding capacity in the vineyard, but the volcanic gravel here is very well drained. It requires very little irrigation and we get smaller berry size and concentrated flavors. The climate, particularly the diurnal swing, brightens the flavors.

WHAT WILL WE NOTICE WHEN TASTING A WINE FROM DIAMOND MOUNTAIN?

All of Diamond Mountain is volcanic in origin. These soils are well drained and mineral-rich. Diamond Mountain wines display the darker fruits. Talking Cabernet, we tend to be more black cherry, currant and blueberry. Plum is also an aroma and flavor I get up here – a different fruit profile. I can't say definitively that it's a result of the volcanic soil or the climate, but it's here.

Tannin balance has been the Holy Grail for winemakers on Diamond Mountain. A lot of our approach has to do with advances in viticulture and winemaking equipment – the fruit exposure and the narrowing of the range of ripeness in the fruit through strategic dropping of fruit, and in the winery, moving away from aggressive pumps and focusing on extraction early in the fermentation. Our wines age well. Diamond Creek started making wines in the late 1960s, and their older wines are superb.

WHAT DO PEOPLE MISUNDERSTAND ABOUT YOUR AVA?

Early on, the wines of Diamond Mountain gained a reputation for being extremely tannic. Advances in both grape growing and winemaking have evolved to make wines with ample but supple tannins. Aggressive tannins are now more of a misconception. The other thing that is somewhat challenging is that while there are a lot of Diamond Mountain AVA wines, there aren't a lot of wineries on the mountain. We don't have a place where people can visit.

WHAT DO YOU WANT PEOPLE TO KNOW ABOUT YOUR AVA?

If you look at Napa Valley in general, one of the things that makes it unique is that while it's this very well-defined place, it has more diverse microclimates than anywhere in the world. We have a lot of different soil types and small environments. Diamond Mountain is part of the Mayacamas Range, the mountains that form the western slopes of the Napa Valley. At the south end of the Mayacamas is Mount Veeder, where you get the cooling bay influence. When you move north to Spring Mountain you find more pockets of sedimentary soils and some great Merlot. By the time you get up to Diamond Mountain, there's only volcanic soils. Cabernet Franc does really well and often plays an important role in the blends.

DIAMOND MOUNTAIN

DRIVE THROUGH NAPA

CLIMATE

Moderately warm with lower maximum temperatures and higher minimum temperatures than the valley floor, due to topography and altitude. Temperature stays between 50 to 90 degrees in growing season.

ELEVATION

400 to 2,200 feet.

RAINFALL

40 to 55 inches annually.

SOILS

Residual uplifted soils of volcanic origin, often reddish and very fine-grained, even gritty in texture, composed of both weathered sedimentary material and soil with volcanic origin. Good drainage.

PRINCIPAL VARIETIES & CHARACTERISTICS

Cabernet Sauvignon, Cabernet Franc: firmly structured, rich and fairly tannic when young, with strong blackcurrant, mineral and cedar-y flavors. Less supple and fleshy than valley floor wines, with good aging potential.

▼

Perched high in the Mayacamas Mountains just southwest of Calistoga, this district in northwest Napa Valley has been home to wine grapes since 1868 when Jacob Schram, founder of Schramsberg, planted his first vines. Its soil contains small pieces of volcanic glass, which is how the area got its name.

The Diamond Mountain AVA is defined by the Napa-Sonoma county line on the west, Petrified Forest Road on the north, the 400-foot line of altitude running parallel to Route 29 in the east, and the Spring Mountain AVA to the south. Its highest vineyards can be found at 2,200 feet above sea level, putting them well above the fog line. They receive more sunlight than vineyards in most other areas of the valley, but the porous volcanic soil allows the vines to cool down quickly after the sun goes down.

Diamond Mountain's topography and altitude combine to give it consistent year-round temperatures and a diurnal swing that is narrower than most other Napa regions.

THE WINERIES HERE CONCENTRATE MAINLY ON CABERNET SAUVIGNON AND CABERNET FRANC. GRAPES TEND TO BE RICH AND TANNIC WITH GOOD ACIDITY; THEY AGE EXCEPTIONALLY WELL.

Diamond Mountain's principal varieties are well structured, quite tannic when young, and give off strong flavors of cedar and blackberry as well as a mineral quality.

MALBEC, MERLOT, PETIT VERDOT AND SAUVIGNON BLANC ARE ALSO PRODUCED HERE.

▼

—

PRICE TO RATING CHART

THE GRAPH INDICATES VIVINO USERS'
AVERAGE RATINGS FOR WINES AT
DIFFERENT PRICE POINTS IN
THIS AVA.

DATA POWERED BY VIVINO

DIAMOND MOUNTAIN

PRICE TO RATING CHART

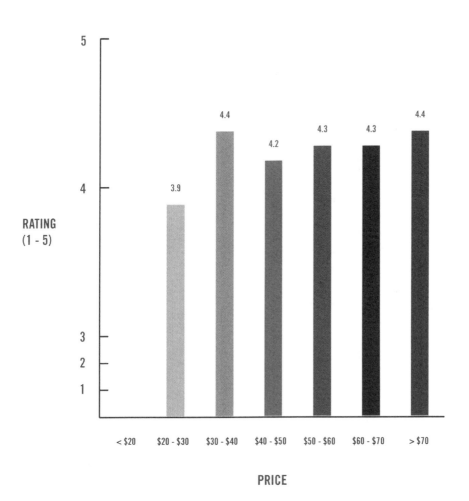

SOUTH TO NORTH

AVA 16:

CALISTOGA

CALISTOGA
WINERIES & VINEYARDS

Amici Cellars
August Briggs Winery
Barlow Vineyards
Bennett Lane Winery
Bragg Vineyards
CAMi Vineyards
Canard Vineyard
Castello di Amorosa
Chateau Montelena
Clos Pegase Wineery
Coquerel Family Wine Estates
Davis Estates
Dutch Henry
Eisele Vineyard
Envy Wines
Fairwinds Estate Winery
Girard Winery
Heritage School Vineyards Winery
Hindsight Wines
Hourglass
Huge Bear Wines
Jack Brooks Vineyard
Jax Vineyards
Jericho Canyon Vineyard
Kenefick Ranch
La Jota Vineyard Co.
La Sirena Wines
Larkmead Vineyards
Mt. Brave
Next Door Wine
Olabisi Winery
Paoletti Estates Winery
Peter Michael Winery
Phifer Pavitt Wine
Poggi Wines
Romeo Vineyards and Cellars
Sebright Cellars
Sterling Vineyards
Storybook Mountain Vineyards
Summers Estate Wines

Tamber Bey Vineyards
Terra Testa Vines
Tom Eddy Winery
Twomey Cellars Winery
Voros Cellars
Weppler Vineyards
Ziata Wines

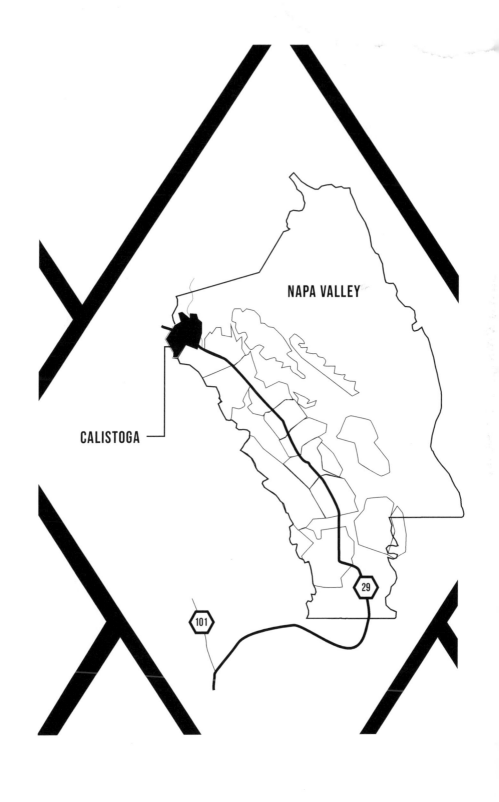

A Q & A —

CALISTOGA

CHATEAU MONTELENA WINERY

BO BARRETT

CEO

WHAT DO YOU LIKE MOST ABOUT CALISTOGA?

One of the unique things about Calistoga is that it's so high. It starts at 300 feet (above sea level). It farms as an extension of the mountains. It's much colder up here than people think, especially at night. More frost protection is needed. The valley is narrow at this point. Most of the Calistoga vineyards are on these alluvial fans, which are big and very deep because the canyons are steep.

WHAT EFFECT DOES THE CALISTOGA AVA HAVE ON THE GRAPES THAT GROW HERE?

Harvest takes longer here. Our Cabernet on the hillsides is ready the earliest. Down in the cold spots, where we do frost protection, we have to be more patient. The soils are pretty sparse, so the crop loads are a little bit lighter. Hillsides can go from 1.5 to 1.65 (tons per acre). In the alluvial fans, we're lucky to get 2.5 tons. Compared to areas south in the valley, we're only about 60 to 70 percent of their yield. That means good intensity.

Fog isn't an issue. The valley turns 25 degrees to the west as it goes north, so the Russian River has a greater effect on us than the marine effect from the south.

▼

WHAT WILL WE NOTICE WHEN TASTING A WINE FROM YOUR AVA?

The vineyard flavor is unique in Calistoga. The wines are typically stronger in their varietal characteristics – a very pronounced concentration of the varietal. On the palate they can be a little bit rough when they're young. Typically a young wine from Calistoga has similar characteristics to a young wine from Howell Mountain: strong and punchy. They have a lot of what I call mountain focus. You have to wait a little while to get a bit more of the softness. That is also a hallmark of this region.

Our wines are definitely made to age. I'd say that our wines age as well as any wine from any place in the world.

WHAT DO PEOPLE MISUNDERSTAND ABOUT YOUR AVA?

What's special and different about Calistoga is the integration of the town with the winemaking community.

We've always been a welcoming community in this little hamlet and it has never had that anti-tourist vibe. Calistoga also has its natural geothermal spas that add to the visitors' fun. You don't really see that elsewhere. It's more like a European wine and spa village where the town is centered on wine, but the place isn't only all about the winemaking. There are little shops in town, things to do and mud baths to take!

Some people don't make the drive all the way up here, which is a shame, because it's very beautiful and close to everything else in Napa. The vistas here, with the combination of the dramatic Palisades, vineyards and tree cover, are breathtaking.

CALISTOGA

DRIVE THROUGH NAPA

CLIMATE

Because of the cool marine air drawn into the valley from the northwestern hills, Calistoga's summertime diurnal swing is the most extreme in Napa Valley. Cool afternoon and evening breezes are the conduit for the ocean air; on clear nights they're reinforced by cold breezes sliding down the mountainsides.

ELEVATION

300 to 1,200 feet.

RAINFALL

Up to 60 inches annually. The highest elevations of this AVA are generally the wettest part of Napa.

SOILS

Almost completely of volcanic origin, soils range from rocky, stony loam on the hillsides to gravelly or cobbly loams on the alluvial fans, and heavier clay-silt soils in the valley center areas.

PRINCIPAL VARIETIES & CHARACTERISTICS

Cabernet Sauvignon, Zinfandel, Syrah, Petite Sirah: Often highly concentrated and exhibiting typical varietal characteristics. Can be rough and unfinished when young, but they age nicely.

▼

In the 19th century Calistoga's hot springs were a tourist draw, and it was their presence that enticed the first entrepreneurs to the area. Samuel Brannan, a successful businessman and journalist who founded San Francisco's first newspaper, wanted to promote the region as a California version of Saratoga Springs, so he devised a huckster's name for marketing purposes: "Calistoga" is a mash-up of "California" and "Saratoga."

Generally, average temperatures rise as you head north in Napa Valley. The Calistoga AVA, situated in the valley's northerly reaches, often experiences daytime highs of well over 100 degrees. But several factors moderate that heat. The porous volcanic soil cools down quickly after sundown because the nearby Russian River and a pronounced marine influence from low points in the hills to the northwest can lower nocturnal temperatures dramatically. As a result, this region can have an unusually large diurnal swing of 50 degrees or more in the summer.

WINE GRAPES WERE FIRST PLANTED HERE AROUND 1852.

Thirty years later, San Francisco businessman Alfred L. Tubbs established what would become one of California's most influential wineries: Chateau Montelena.

Through that winery's long-term efforts, Calistoga became an important AVA, though surprisingly it wasn't formed until 2010. It's one of Napa's fastest-growing wine regions, partly because it developed later than other areas due to its northerly location.

IN THE LAST 25 YEARS THE NUMBER OF WINERIES HERE HAS MORE THAN DOUBLED FROM 13 TO ABOUT 30.

Most vineyards in the Calistoga appellation are planted on slopes and hillsides rather than the valley floor, laid out between 300 and 1,200 feet above sea level. Calistoga owns an interesting statistic: the highest ratio of steep slopes to valley floor of any Napa AVA. And unlike most Napa AVAs, its soil composition is remarkably consistent – it's all volcanic bedrock and sediments, though it can vary from rocky to silty in texture. This consistency, together with the uniform climate throughout the AVA, takes a certain amount of guesswork out of growing grapes here.

The fairly abundant precipitation means that dry farming is feasible in years with normal rainfall.

One attractive feature of the area for visitors is its relative isolation and the absence of much retail development. It feels more like Sonoma than Napa sometimes.

—

PRICE TO RATING CHART

THE GRAPH INDICATES VIVINO USERS'
AVERAGE RATINGS FOR WINES AT
DIFFERENT PRICE POINTS IN
THIS AVA.

DATA POWERED BY VIVINO

CALISTOGA

PRICE TO RATING CHART

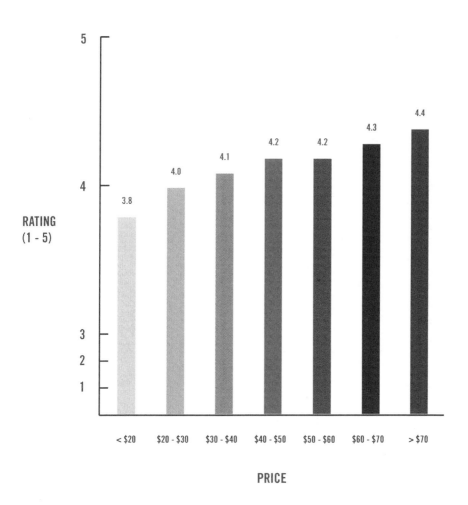

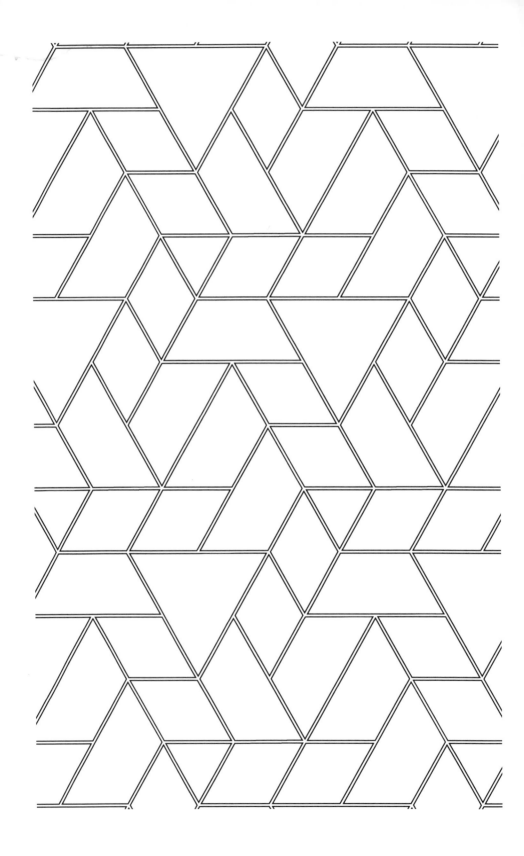

A & Q -

ANDY
ERICKSON

▼

A RARE & MAGICAL PLACE

A LEGENDARY WINEMAKER REVEALS WHAT MAKES NAPA GREAT

Perhaps no winemaker embodies the style and spirit of Napa like Andy Erickson. His 25-year career has taken him to America's most iconic and celebrated wineries, and he is responsible for some of the valley's most passionately sought after bottles.

Erickson came to Napa in 1994 after working for several years in advertising in San Francisco. After working at Stag's Leap Wine Cellars and Newton Vineyard, he enrolled at UC Davis, receiving a graduate degree in enology while working with Spottswoode and Saintsbury wineries. Over the next decade he was associated with three spectacular labels: Harlan Estate, Staglin Family Vineyards and Screaming Eagle. Dalla Valle and Ovid are also on his resume.

Currently, when he's not consulting, Erickson spends much of his time at the winery he founded with his wife, Favia Erickson Winegrowers, in Coombsville.

WE SELECTED ERICKSON TO ANSWER SOME FUNDAMENTAL QUESTIONS ABOUT NAPA VALLEY AND WHY IT HAS EARNED ITS PLACE AMONG THE WORLD'S GREAT WINE REGIONS.

▼

WHY IS NAPA A WORLD-CLASS PRODUCER OF WINE? WHAT UNIQUE CONDITIONS MAKE IT SO SUCCESSFUL?

It's a combination of many things – volcanic soils, proximity to the cooling breezes of the Pacific Ocean, diversity of geography and geology, the simplicity of the valley – it's very easy for lots of people to come here, cover the whole place, and quickly grasp it. Napa attracts serious wine connoisseurs as well as the more casual fans.

The diurnal swing is huge here – in some places it's 100 degrees during the day and 50 at night. The climate is stable compared to the winemaking areas of Europe. We get some weather in the winter, but in the summer it's gorgeous; it rarely rains. And we can irrigate here. All in all the weather is quite predictable, which is a valuable asset.

WHAT CHANGES HAVE YOU SEEN IN THE LAST 25 YEARS?

When I started in '94 I worked in the cellar right away. Back then, winemakers were still emulating what was being done in Bordeaux. But over the last 20-plus years we've decided we have something special to offer here – something unlike anywhere else in the world. We are still finding the right ways to express it. There is always fine-tuning to be done. We're always working on defining what is the Napa style of wine.

Bordeaux varieties are clearly the best way to express it, but it depends on style. People are beginning to look for more balance in wines. That means more balanced vineyards.

DO YOU HAVE ANY SUGGESTIONS FOR THOSE VISITING THE NAPA VALLEY FOR THE FIRST TIME?

I would tell them to look at Napa as a collection of individual appellations as opposed to one big appellation. Learning how to differentiate the small AVAs is very helpful. Napa does have little nooks and crannies, and it's fun to explore the valley in that way – get off the beaten track. The more you explore, the more you learn. It's fascinating to taste the differences between wine from Mount Veeder vs. Oakville vs. Coombsville. Pay attention to geology and soil and the mountains. There are so many variables governing each vineyard.

WHAT TRENDS ARE YOU SEEING IN YOUR BUSINESS, ESPECIALLY THOSE THAT PERTAIN TO NAPA?

Once they get pretty far into their research, wine fans like the idea of terroir and what makes a certain site unique. To express the site, the winemaker needs to be careful about extraction and how ripe the fruit is. I think that people are looking for more balanced wines as well. You know, balance is a pretty subjective word. The pendulum swung one way in Napa for a long time.

Wines were big and overripe. Now everyone is pulling the pendulum the other way. I think the best wines are neither over- or under-expressive, but in the middle.

SELF-TAUGHT WINEMAKERS SEEM TO BE DISAPPEARING. HOW IMPORTANT TO YOUR CAREER WAS YOUR GRADUATE WORK IN ENOLOGY?

I think it's probably more important than some people would think. I'd say that by three years into my career, it was pretty clear there was a lot I didn't know on a technical level. So I went back to school and got my master's. Sure, there are a lot of tools in the toolbox that I don't use all the time. And there are plenty of people who are making good wine without university degrees. There is a network of consultants, myself included, that will troubleshoot for people. That's the thing, you don't really need that knowledge until something goes wrong. If you're young you might not have a difficult time for years. But I'm glad I have the training; sooner or later, everyone needs it.

SOME PEOPLE GRUMBLE ABOUT THE EXTENT OF DEVELOPMENT IN NAPA VALLEY AND THE RISE OF TOURISM. HOW DO YOU FEEL ABOUT WINE-INDUSTRY GENTRIFICATION?

It's definitely a concern. It's something we talk about all the time. I'm on the board of the Napa Valley Vintners, and I joined for that reason. Napa at its core is an agricultural community. We really do need to manage tourism the right way. Obviously we need people to come and buy our wines, but I think growing grapes and making wine are absolutely the primary purpose of the county, and tourism needs to be managed with that in mind.

WHAT DOES THE FUTURE HOLD FOR NAPA?

You will see continued proliferation of AVAs. In Oakville, for example, to me it's at least three different appellations, maybe more. An area between Coombsville and Stags Leap is still undefined. Along the eastern foothills of Atlas Peak, a lot of areas have their own character. In that sense, Napa is very young. It's still discovering itself.

▼

—

PRICE TO RATING CHART

THE GRAPH INDICATES VIVINO USERS'
AVERAGE RATINGS FOR WINES AT
DIFFERENT PRICE POINTS IN
THIS AVA.

DATA POWERED BY VIVINO

NAPA COUNTY

PRICE TO RATING CHART

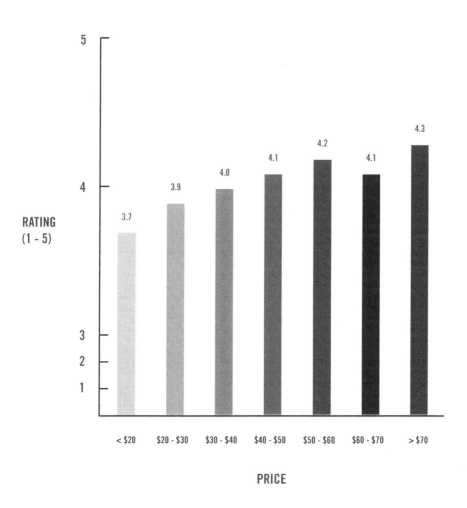

**RATING
(1 - 5)**

Price	Rating
< $20	3.7
$20 - $30	3.9
$30 - $40	4.0
$40 - $50	4.1
$50 - $60	4.2
$60 - $70	4.1
> $70	4.3

PRICE

BIBLIO-GRAPHY

Bonne, Jon, The New California Wine:
A Guide to the Producers and Wines Behind a
Revolution in Taste (Ten Speed Press, 2013)

Insight Editions, Napa Valley Cabernets: The
Best of California's Wine Country (Insight, 2016)

Lewin, Benjamin, Napa Valley and Sonoma
(Guides to Wines and Top Vineyards)
(Vendange Press, 2018)

Pinney, Thomas, A History of Wine in America,
Volume 1: From the Beginnings to Prohibition
(University of California Press, 1989)

Sullivan, Charles L., Napa Wine: A History
from Mission Days to Present, second edition
(The Wine Appreciation Guild, 2008)

Statistics on Napa appellations and other
information sourced with permission from
the website of Napa Valley Vintners
(napavintners.com)

PAUL HODGINS

Paul Hodgins earned a doctorate in music from the University of Southern California and was a professor of dance at UC Irvine before switching careers to journalism, where his arts reviews and wine writing have won several awards and honors. Paul's book on Paso Robles was published in 2017.

KATHY LAJVARDI

Award-winning artist Kathy Lajvardi graduated from Otis College of Art and Design and found immediate success in advertising, film and entertainment. She has worked with Madonna and Beyonce, and her graphics appeared in the movie trailers for Iron Man and Transformers. Her paintings and photographs have been featured at a dozen major galleries. http://kathylajvardi.com

NAUSHAD HUDA

Chicago native Naushad Huda is the founder of I Like This Grape, a digital publication that makes wine relatable to modern audiences. He also co-founded XTOPOLY, a strategy agency, then sold it to devote his time to the pursuit of vino. He lives in Laguna Beach with his wife, Kathy, and two daughters. naushad@ilikethisgrape.com